THE
PSYCHOTHERAPY
MAZE

THE PSYCHOTHERAPY MAZE

A Consumer's Guide to the Ins and Outs of Therapy

Otto Ehrenberg

and

Miriam Ehrenberg

Holt, Rinehart and Winston
New York

Published simultaneously in Canada by Holt, Rinehart
and Winston of Canada, Limited.

Library of Congress Cataloging in Publication Data
Ehrenberg, Otto.
The psychotherapy maze.
Bibliography: p.
Includes index.
1. Psychotherapy. 2. Psychotherapy–Evaluation.
I. Ehrenberg, Miriam, joint author. II. Title.
[DNLM: 1. Psychotherapy–Popular works.
2. Physician–Patient relations–Popular works.
3. Consumer satisfaction–Popular works. WM20 E31p]
RC480.E37   616.8'914   77–71350
ISBN 0–03–016886–4
ISBN 0–03–022881–6 pbk.

Chapter 9 of this book appeared in somewhat altered form
in *New York* magazine, May 12, 1975.

First Edition
Designer: Robert Aulicino
Printed in the United States of America
1 3 5 7 9 10 8 6 4 2

To
Ingrid and *Erica*

We would like to thank Lynn Caine, who insisted on the importance of this book and encouraged us to write it; James H. Endlsey for reading the original article from which this book stemmed and suggesting ways of making it more useful to readers; and Vivienne W. Nearing, our sister, friend, and attorney, for her expert counsel all along the way. It was a delight for us to work with our editor, Marian Wood, whose intelligent and sensitive suggestions helped to make this a better book.

Since we wanted to look at psychotherapy not only with the eyes of therapists but with the eyes of clients as well, we interviewed many people about their psychotherapy experiences during the course of writing this book. They offered freely of their time to help us and, more importantly, to help others who are concerned about psychotherapy. Many thanks to all.

Contents

1.
To Go or Not to Go

ONCE ASSOCIATED IN THE PUBLIC MIND WITH THE ALLE-viation of emotional problems, psychotherapy is now seen as the road to self-fulfillment and joy. Psychotherapeutic theories, techniques, and practitioners have proliferated, holding out the hope of freedom from problems along with the promise of emotional growth. New books on self-assertion, being your own best friend, or learning how to say no are constantly finding their way to the best-seller lists, and the classified sections of newspapers and magazines offer a variety of encounter groups, transactional groups, feminist therapy, primal therapy, or growth therapy, among others. Psychotherapy has not only become big business, it has become one of the steadiest growth industries in the country. More and more practitioners, trained and untrained, competent and incompetent, are flocking to the field. The result, for the public, has been an ever-increasing state of confusion and uncertainty in which abuses flourish.

In such a climate, the psychotherapy consumer needs guidelines and protection. The high risks in psychotherapy make it just as necessary to establish consumer rights in this field as in law, medicine, or automotive repair. People have, and should have, questions about what psychotherapy can and cannot do for them. Rather than responding to these legitimate questions, the tendency among practitioners has been to ignore such concerns and to put clients on the defensive for voicing them. It is often assumed that clients, as lay persons, have no basis for evaluating either the credentials of psychotherapists or the effectiveness of their own therapy. Many psychotherapy systems have built into them a "client trap": the psychotherapist, as the expert, knows the client better than the client knows him/herself and, therefore, the client must accept as correct what the therapist says. If the client agrees with the therapist, that proves the therapist is right. If the client disagrees with the therapist, that also proves the therapist is right because the client's resistance reveals the therapist has hit target. The therapist, being the expert on interpersonal relationships, is defined as healthy, always acting in a proper way, and above being questioned by one who is "neurotic," "sick," or "paranoid."

Clients have traditionally been relegated to the underdog position in the psychotherapy relationship, thereby perpetuating a fundamentally countertherapeutic attitude. This attitude has fostered intimidation rather than emancipation and growth. If you are in psychotherapy or about to take the plunge, you can protect yourself from authoritarian therapists, quacks, needless therapy, excessive costs, and other abuses. It is not only your right but your responsibility as a psychotherapy client to look after your self-interests. To get the most out of psychotherapy you must know what is reasonable to expect and unreasonable to accept. Awareness of what the process entails—its scope as well as its limitations—provides the basis for a meaningful psychotherapy experience.

What Psychotherapy Is All About

How do you know if your problems belong in a psychotherapist's office? Everyone experiences discomfort, stress, and strain at one point or another. Some people, because of the realities of their life situations, are faced with more problems than others, but that still does not mean that they should go into psychotherapy. Psychotherapy does not eliminate the difficulties of living, nor is it by itself a solution when the external conditions of life are so oppressive that you are not free to exercise any options in dealing with your problems. When you have no money to live on you need a job, not treatment for your insecurity. But when you are afraid to go on a job interview because you feel inadequate or are sure beforehand that someone else will be hired, you should consider psychotherapy. Psychotherapy is called for when the restrictions come from within yourself, when you do not feel free to face life's difficulties in constructive ways.

People bring a variety of problems to psychotherapy. Some suffer from disabling anxiety attacks or headaches, some from compulsive habits such as excessive drinking or overeating, some from feelings of worthlessness or depression, some from inability to have relationships. Others do not feel particularly troubled but feel that life is empty and unsatisfying. Psychotherapy's immediate concern is helping people overcome these problems and the unhappiness they cause. But psychotherapy is also aware that these problems stem from a common base. In each condition the person is not free to live productively and not free to be him/herself. While this lack of freedom manifests itself differently in different people, it is always the fundamental issue for psychotherapy.

Psychotherapy recognizes that each person has the innate capacity to grow, to know oneself, and to make choices consonant with the development of one's potential. Growth— the unfolding of one's core—is a natural condition of being alive and is synonymous with psychological well-being. Conversely, when growth is blocked and one is not free to be oneself, a person experiences an inner sense of disharmony. Psychotherapy explores the ways people limit their lives and undermine their autonomy. By revealing obstacles to growth, psychotherapy can help free people from self-restricting attitudes and patterns of behavior and bring nascent qualities to the fore. In helping people live up to the responsibility for self-realization that being human demands, psychotherapy is essentially a moral enterprise.

The process of psychotherapy must be compatible with its goal of expanding your autonomy. It is not a process where the psychotherapist "cures" you or does something to you. Rather, it is a collaborative educational process based on your active participation. The therapist's role is not that of a doctor but of teacher who acts as catalyst and guide in your efforts to understand the ways in which you hinder your own development and avoid possibilities for growth. The therapist must help you expose the ways you flee from your own affirmation and also help you gain control over your existence. The psychotherapist must not validate your fears of help-

4 THE PSYCHOTHERAPY MAZE

lessness and powerlessness by doing things for you that you can do for yourself. Any process in which you relinquish responsibility for growth to the therapist is not authentic psychotherapy.

Much of the confusion about the methods and aims of psychotherapy stems from the erroneous classification of emotional problems as "mental illness." Unlike a bodily illness, which is something tangible that you have, a "mental illness" is a way of being—something that you are. Guilts, anxieties, and hostilities are not diseases that can be cured but feelings that have to be confronted and understood. You can not "cure" the way you are, you can only change the way you are. Some therapy techniques ignore this central issue and focus instead on treating symptoms. Alleviating the symptom —the anxiety, the shyness, the depression, the sexual dysfunction—offers temporary relief, but does not solve the problem that brought it about. It is a way to help you get along the way you are, not a way to help you grow and change. Masking the problem and reducing its impact through symptomatic treatment is only a stopgap measure. In the long run, treating symptoms will help you only if it does not avoid the problems of living, but instead facilitates solving those problems.

Goals and Expectations

Whether or not you decide to go into psychotherapy, and the type of psychotherapy you seek, will be influenced by your expectations and goals. The array of approaches before you is enormous. Psychotherapy and related services can be used in various ways, to various degrees, and toward various ends: to overcome disturbing mental states, to lift disabling symptoms, to provide help with a particular problem, or to search for more open ways of living.

The chances of success in psychotherapy will be greater the more the choice of therapy and therapist is compatible with your needs, goals, and life situation. You are free to ask for what you want, but you also have the obligation to yourself not to request or accept that which violates your integrity. Not everything that makes you feel good is ultimately in your best interest. Tranquilizers can calm you down, but they can also lead to habituation. Letting the therapist make your decisions for you may be temporarily reassuring, but it also undermines your confidence in your own capacities. Such interventions are a potential hazard in that they invite an outside agent to take over for you, and the comfort they provide can seduce you into compromising your basic need for independence. You must weigh the demands of authentic psychotherapy against the final goals. The broader the goals, the more psychotherapy has to offer, and the more life will have to offer.

Psychotherapy is a challenging and exciting life-expanding undertaking. Like all such ventures, it places demands on you. You have to be ready to deal with things you would rather forget, to keep working even when you do not seem to be making much progress, and to tolerate the anxiety of putting your new understanding into action. Psychotherapy takes time, effort, and courage.

It might be difficult for you to accept the demanding aspects of psychotherapy, especially if you start while very distressed. When you are feeling extremely anxious or depressed, you want to feel better fast. You want somebody to take care of you and get you over the hump. The therapist will be sorely tempted to settle for giving you what you want at the moment: to patch you up with moral support, advice, or a tranquilizer and send you home happy for a while. This kind of care may make you feel better, and it may be a needed step to put you in a frame of mind to be ready to face your problems, but it is not psychotherapy. The ability to resolve this conflict between wanting to be cared for and learning how to care for yourself is a crucial factor in avoiding disappointments in psychotherapy.

You cannot expect psychotherapy to take all your troubles away. Psychotherapy does not eliminate life's problems, but it does help you to face up to them. It cannot make hostile, competitive, or overly demanding people in your life disappear any more than it can make social evils disappear, but it can give you the means to deal with these and other problems of life in a more productive way, and in a way that modifies the external situations. The more competent and determined you are in your approach to the world, the greater the possibilities that it will accommodate itself to you. Psychotherapy can provide the basis for greater happiness by opening up new ways of existing and enlarging on the choices you will feel free to make.

Obstacles to Psychotherapy

Only a small proportion of people for whom psycho-therapy could be useful ever go to a psychotherapist. To start psychotherapy, one not only has to have an appreciation of what it has to offer but also to overcome fears about the process and cultural prejudices against it.

Inner Fears Going into psychotherapy means, first of all, facing up to personal shortcomings. Many people con-sider it demeaning to have problems in living, problems they seem unable to cope with, and are reluctant to admit that they do, even to themselves. Since most people who start psychotherapy have poor self-esteem, it is particularly threat-ening for them to acknowledge their difficulties. Recognizing one's limitations is made even more difficult by the habit of labeling people with emotional problems as "sick." Nobody wants the stigma of mental illness. A related stumbling block to psychotherapy is the reluctance to reveal things about one-self that carry a sense of shame. In a mistrustful society, it is worrisome to think of exposing yourself to others. The cul-ture is also critical of people talking about their problems; you are supposed to keep a stiff upper lip and not be "weak." This attitude makes it especially difficult for men to start psychotherapy because they fear that it will mark them as "unmasculine."

Another fear, also more common among men, is that psychotherapy means surrendering independence. People are afraid that they may become too needy of the psychotherapist. Some psychotherapists do foster dependency by encouraging clients to rely on them rather than on inner resources, but this is not inevitable. Authentic psychotherapy always aims at developing your independence and ability to take responsi-bility for your own life. On the other hand, some people are scared away by this very striving for self-responsibility. They do not want this responsibility, preferring that others con-tinue to take care of them. Even though it is uncomfortable to have problems, they can still count on indulgence from others: "Don't bother me—I can't cope."

Still others are afraid to start psychotherapy because they are not sure they are up to the task. They doubt their ability to participate meaningfully in the therapy process or their potential for change. They fear a further exposure of their inadequacy. Their feelings of worthlessness may also make them afraid of rejection by the therapist.

Some people fear that psychotherapy can cause a loss of creativity. This concern is based on a popular misconception that creative persons are "neurotic" and that eliminating the neurosis will make them "normal" and dull. Since the essential qualities of the genuine creative act—openness and spontaneity—are also basic goals of psychotherapy, psychotherapy is more apt to liberate than to block creative forces.

An increasing number of people, especially those with radical political views, shy away from psychotherapy because they think the goal of therapy is to make them adjust to the status quo. Psychotherapy does, indeed, have political implications and can be a repressive political act, as R. D. Laing and many others have pointed out. It may or may not be the intention of the psychotherapist to have the client conform to societal values, and this is an issue to be explored with a therapist before working together. At times, psychotherapists unwittingly use therapy as a tool of conformity when they are unaware of repressive cultural influences from which clients need to free themselves. However, labeling all psychotherapists as upholders of the establishment may be a smoke screen that keeps a person from having to take a closer look at his/her own problems.

Still other doubts about psychotherapy revolve around its time and cost. The recent spate of such methods as encounter, marathon, and sensitivity groups, assertiveness training, and *est*, attest to the desire for quicker and less costly routes to self-development. For some people, such approaches have been helpful, but for others these attempts to bypass the more encompassing process of psychotherapy have been woefully unsuccessful and, at times, even harmful.

Outer Barriers   Apart from these personal hurdles, various social influences discourage a serious psychotherapeutic effort. Paradoxically, a frequent barrier results from the needs of close friends and relatives. Although these same people may initially push a person into psychotherapy, they often become its enemy instead of its advocate. If they find it hard to accept the growing independence of the person in therapy, they begin to struggle against it. Interactions with others are a two-way process and changes in the patterning have repercussions with which everyone must contend. The woman who realizes that her "pussycat" role is degrading cannot discard the décolleté and dish towel without resistance on the part of her mate. The son who rejects his mother's sacrifices to be rid of the accompanying guilt may find that she refuses to forsake her martyrdom. It may even happen that friends and relatives become jealous of the therapist's influence on the person in therapy.

The cultural climate also functions as a barrier to psychotherapy. A pervasive theme of the culture is the veneration of quick and easy routes to feeling good. We are urged to take aspirin for "fast, fast, fast relief," antihistamines "at the first sign of a cold," and tablets for "sweet and easy sleep, sleep, sleep." We want a quick cure for our discomfort, being seduced by the easy way out and blinded to its dangers. A climate that embraces all convenience items despite their dangerous side effects—aerosol cans, birth control pills, instant foods, plastic wraps—hardly promotes a willingness to engage in a process, like psychotherapy, that may prove arduous and long.

In still more fundamental ways, society discourages us from aspiring to more autonomous ways of life. People who are not willing to confine their possibilities for growth are apt to find new pathways that can become menacing to the status quo. Our concept of psychological normalcy is, in fact, culturally defined, with "normal" being behavior that is conventional and "abnormal" being behavior that departs from the usual acceptable social standards. This makes it easier to "adjust" to things the way they are than to risk change and have to buck society.

The push to adjust to society is reinforced even by those professions that are ostensibly devoted to promoting the integrity of the individual. Such "helping professions" as religion, law, medicine, and ofttimes psychotherapy, act as agents of the culture by labeling as immoral, illegal, and abnormal that which is threatening to the status quo. For example, it is not accidental that abortion and homosexuality were immoral and illegal acts when society needed a growing population but became individual "rights" when society needed zero population growth. The professions set the stage for conformity by fostering authoritarian relationships in which the individual is treated like a child, to be protected by a knowledgeable adult: the priest or "father" ministers to his "son" while the "doctor" calls the patient by his first name. One is encouraged to let the professional assume responsibility for essential decisions in one's life. At the extreme is the professional who arrogates the right to decide what information about the client will be disclosed. Physicians, lawyers, and ministers have conspired to keep people unaware that they were suffering from a terminal illness, thereby depriving them of the right to come to terms with their own lives. Psychiatrists have had persons committed involuntarily to mental institutions under the guise of knowing better than their patients what is in the latter's best interest.

The concept of mental illness in itself functions as a barrier to authentic psychotherapy and self-responsibility. As Thomas Szasz points out in *The Myth of Mental Illness*, this concept is testimony to society's unwillingness to let individuals deal with their problems in idiosyncratic ways. In the Middle Ages, persons who could not live according to the rules were condemned as witches. Contemporary deviancy is defined as "mental illness" and "mental patients" are seen as possessed by an illness instead of the devil. To rid them of the illness, they are given insulin or electric shock, drugs, psychosurgery, behavior modification, or token psychotherapy. While the less powerful persons in our society—the lower socioeconomic groups, blacks, and women—are more likely to be institutionalized and given damaging labels, the middle and upper classes are not immune to these dangers. A more socially acceptable label such as "nervous exhaustion" may be applied in their situation, but they still find themselves involuntarily subjected to heavy medication and shock. In putting the treatment of personality problems into the medical domain, the concept of mental illness denies individual responsibility for one's condition. The legal definition of insanity sanctions this view by declaring that insane persons are not responsible for their own acts.

These personal fears and cultural barriers not only make it difficult for people to seek psychotherapy, but also make them start off with wrong attitudes. People are apt to relinquish their authority at the very beginning, expecting the therapist to take over their "treatment." Many come in expecting rapid cures without determined effort on their part. With such attitudes it is not surprising that there are so many disappointments in psychotherapy. These misconceptions need to be dispelled before a genuine therapeutic process can begin to take place.

Does Psychotherapy Work?

With so much at stake in psychotherapy, it is important to know if it really works. Lots of research has been conducted to evaluate effectiveness. The results of these studies show that psychotherapy works, that psychotherapy does not work, and that psychotherapy has harmful effects. These contradictory findings stem from different views of what constitutes success in psychotherapy, different views on how this success is determined, and bias in doing the research. Much of it has been motivated by the desire either to debunk or to defend psychotherapy, to acclaim one new approach or to discredit another.

The first source of confusion in research is the differing determinants of what constitutes success in psychotherapy. Is it removal of a disturbing symptom, achievement of a specific goal, disappearance of problems, greater awareness of oneself, an increase in happiness, or the freedom to make fuller use of life? The varied approaches labeled psychotherapy emphasize different goals. Effectiveness can therefore only be measured against psychotherapy's success in reaching the goals for which it is intended.

The next problem is how to determine whether success has been reached. Does one use the evaluation of therapists, of clients, of family or friends, or of psychological tests? All of these sources have been used, and each presents limitations. The therapist's or client's reports are mistrusted by some because they are considered to be biased, with both therapist and client needing to justify their efforts. Other, presumably more objective, people are not suitable judges since they may not be aware of changes that are significant to the client; and psychological tests often miss the point altogether. Another problem is the point in time when the results of psychotherapy should be measured. Should it be evaluated after two months, a year, after termination, or at a later date? Some therapy systems aim at fairly rapid observable changes, others at laying groundwork for changes that may not become apparent until much later. The effects of therapy do not end when therapy stops: benefits may continue to accrue as insights and changes have a chance to solidify.

With all these variables, the inconsistency of results is not surprising. Moreover, research has been asking the wrong question. With the vast array of psychotherapy approaches, psychotherapists, and clients, the relevant issue is not if psychotherapy works, but which approaches work under what conditions and with whom. Research is now addressing itself to those questions. Even when more definite answers are available, it will still be hard to quantify the benefits of psychotherapy. Sometimes just a little bit of help at the right time can be of immeasurable importance.

Not all systems are beneficial to all people all the time, but there is enough evidence to conclude that some systems are beneficial to some people some of the time. Just how useful psychotherapy will be depends on many factors that are discussed in this book. The most important issues are your motives for going into psychotherapy, your goals in psychotherapy, the type of therapy you choose, the type of therapist you choose, and the way in which you apply yourself in psychotherapy.

Who Should Go into Psychotherapy

People go to psychotherapy for a variety of reasons. Most go because they are seriously distressed and need help coping with day-to-day life. Some are not particularly distressed but go to psychotherapy because they want to get more out of life. Others go because they are curious about psychotherapy or because they want to do the "in" thing. Still others go not really wanting psychotherapy: they want to get reassurance that they are not "crazy," to fix blame on somebody else, or to meet the demands of an authority such as a parent, spouse, school, or probation officer. Sometimes, too, people go to psychotherapy under the pretext that they are doing it for someone else, to camouflage their own interest in doing so. If you are considering psychotherapy, think about your reasons for wanting to go. The more genuinely you want psychotherapy, the more helpful it will be. People who go only at the insistence of others are not really open to the possibilities of exploring themselves or of changing themselves.

Being aware of your discomfort and anxiety is a positive sign. People who are in touch with their feelings rather than blocking them out are already one step ahead in psychotherapy. The more you are aware of your distress and of not being able to be what you want, the stronger will be your desire for change. It is hard to undertake the work of psychotherapy without the longing for growth.

There is a popular saying among psychotherapists that the ideal client for psychotherapy is the person who needs it the least. This ideal type is known as the "yavis": young, attractive, verbal, intelligent, successful. However, these characteristics are not necessary in order to benefit from psychotherapy. The belief in the importance of verbal and intellectual ability is particularly widespread. The ability to put feelings into words can be of value, but verbal facility can just as easily be used to hide one's feelings behind a wall of intellectualization. Furthermore, words are only one way to express yourself. The assumption that the successful intellectual elite benefits the most from psychotherapy has hindered psychotherapy in tapping nonverbal modes of experience and in making itself available to lower socioeconomic groups.

Some therapists feel a "yavis" makes a better client because it is easier for them to establish a good relationship with this type. They prefer to work with such persons and equate their preference with necessary client characteristics.

What really matters in being a client is your interest in psychotherapy. Psychotherapy is helpful only to those who really want help. It can benefit all people who are willing to expend the effort to make meaningful changes.

Getting Started

It's not easy to get started in psychotherapy. There is the uncertainty about how to go about doing it: how do you pick a therapist, what do you say when you go to one, and what do you have to do once you're in therapy? You probably feel anxious about starting off on a new experience in which a lot is at stake and the outcome uncertain. You are not sure what is going to happen to you, and how you are going to take to it. You might be worried about what other people are going to think of you. On top of all this, you have to overcome a certain amount of lethargy. Getting started means putting in time and effort, it means planning, committing yourself to a new routine, and it usually means having to make financial sacrifices.

With these attitudes to overcome, there is a tendency to put off starting therapy until stress and discomfort force you to act. But waiting till then puts you at a disadvantage: you will have lost the freedom to look around for a suitable therapist, wanting instead to latch on to the first one you come across. When you are very upset your emotional resources become dissipated, leaving you less capacity to work at the therapy. And, the longer you wait, the more your problems and reactions to them become crystallized, making it that much harder to bring about changes.

Getting started is easier the clearer you are on what kind of therapy you want and how to go about getting it. This will narrow down the possibilities to manageable proportions and eliminate obviously inappropriate approaches. With a framework in mind for judging the suitability of therapists, you won't feel so overwhelmed about the choices you'll have to make.

Don't feel intimidated by the therapists you meet. Keep in mind your role vis-à-vis the therapist. Even though the therapist is the expert, you are the client, the one who is buying a service. Not only do you have a right to question the therapist, but you have the responsibility to yourself to get what you want and need. Don't worry about the impression you are making on the therapist. What is important is the impression that the therapist makes on you. If you are unsure about a therapist, look around for someone else. If you make a bad choice, it is not a binding decision. You can always quit and try again.

2.
The Major Approaches

PSYCHOTHERAPY IS ONLY ONE OF MANY APPROACHES TO personal problems and emotional difficulties. Other techniques are often used as adjuncts to psychotherapy or as alternates to psychotherapy. Often these are confused with psychotherapy, but they can be distinguished in several ways. Psychotherapy, unlike other techniques, focuses on expanding client awareness and autonomy. It assumes that self-awareness and the ability to make informed choices are the basis of psychological growth and well-being. The psychotherapist works in a close relationship with the client to help the client help him/herself. Other techniques view the client as someone suffering from an unwanted symptom or behavioral pattern that will be removed for him/her. Control of the therapy process and responsibility for change is put in the hands of the therapist rather than the client. This chapter summarizes the major psychotherapy approaches as well as other prominent approaches, including behavior therapy and medical treatment, which do not fit into the definition of psychotherapy used here.

In addition to the distinction between psychotherapy and other techniques, there are many different approaches within psychotherapy itself. As the world has changed, psychotherapy has changed to meet the new needs and interests that have emerged. A discernible trend has been a shift in focus from personal problems to interpersonal problems and now toward transpersonal problems. The new approaches, in keeping with the tempo of the times, emphasize immediate awareness in lieu of worked-through insight. Accordingly, the pitfalls of psychotherapy have shifted from "interminable" psychoanalysis to the substitution of apparent for real gains.

With the advent of mass media there has also been a dramatic change in the way psychotherapy systems come into being. Formerly, new systems were built up painstakingly and offered bit by bit to the professional community; now, new systems are promoted on a mass basis and burgeon overnight. Innovators do not look for the approval of their colleagues but take their wares directly to the public marketplace. Books on psychotherapy are at the top of the best-seller lists and television popularizes the faces of all the latter-day psychotherapy inventors. As a result, fads in psychotherapy take hold much as new products, with new therapy systems giving way to still newer "brands" every few years. The charisma of a therapist on television often becomes more important than the soundness of his/her system and visibility becomes confused with validity.

The multitude of schools of psychotherapy is taken by some to indicate that psychotherapy is not a valid body of knowledge but a conglomeration of unproven theories, some brilliant, some far-out, and some just plain stupid. If psychotherapists really know what they are about, how come they all disagree, and if psychotherapy is a bona fide process, is that process psychoanalysis, primal screaming, or a nondirective "uh-huh"? A lot of the confusion comes about from the fact that different theoreticians focus on different human psychological phenomena. Each theoretician presents a system based on the distillation of his/her own personal experiences, and those of the persons he/she deals with as revealed in their relationships. None of the theories is completely right or wrong; each reflects on a certain set of approaches to the world. Knowing which theory is most suitable to you is less important than recognizing that no theory will properly account for all your experiences: they have yet to be explored within the psychotherapy process. Your psychotherapy should be the revelation of the principles and laws of your life instead of an imposition of a set of principles on you. This may be better facilitated in one system rather than another, but no one system that is rigidly applied can possibly do you justice. The more a therapist holds to a particular theory, the more danger that he/she will not be able to hear what you are saying. Therapists who have found all the answers are not capable of hearing what does not fit into their preconceived ideas. Dogmatic adherence to any theory leaves the client high and dry.

The psychotherapy systems summarized here vary in several ways:

- Some focus on promoting growth, others on removing symptoms
- Some focus on cooperative work, others on therapist control
- Some focus on internal dynamics, others on relationships with the environment
- Some focus on past development, others on present functioning
- Some focus on experiencing feelings, others on developing understanding

Despite different emphases, in practice psychotherapies turn out to be more similar than dissimilar. Differences in theoretical approach seem to have less of an impact than differences in therapist personality. Experienced psychotherapists tend to behave in similar ways. Good therapists sense the limitations of the particular theories they subscribe to and reach out to clients in ways that cut across theoretical differences. Therapists who do not know how to respond in spontaneous ways are more rigid in sticking to a theory. Though therapists have preferences among the various theories, many are eclectic in the sense that they are not exclusively committed to any one system. They modify their approach depending on the client's problems, responsiveness, or stage in therapy. Even between psychotherapy and other approaches, a cross-semination takes place. Quite a few psychotherapists use behavior therapy or medical treatment as adjuncts to the psychotherapy process, and adherents of those therapies are starting to incorporate psychotherapeutic approaches.

Choose a theoretical approach that makes sense to you and deals with problems as you experience them. Don't get stuck with an approach that distorts your experience in order to uphold the validity of the theory. The brief review of theoretical approaches that follows is intended as an introduction; for those interested, further reading is suggested at the end of this book.

Freud and Psychoanalysis

Freudian therapy is the most widely known and has been around the longest. Psychotherapy as we know it today started with Freud who both enunciated a theory of personality development and developed a therapeutic technique known as psychoanalysis. The personality theory is "Freudian," while the technique is "psychoanalytic," which is why there is confusion as to what psychoanalysis really means. To Freudian adherents, it means a technique that utilizes Freud's theory of personality; but to others, it means a technique of depth analysis that can interpret behavior according to other theoretical assumptions.

According to Freud, people are motivated by their instincts, the sexual instinct being the most basic. The instincts are always seeking gratification but their demands must be modified because of the realities of life, including moral restrictions. The personality is organized into three parts: the id, which represents the instinctual needs; the ego, which tries to satisfy the id according to the reality situation; and the superego, which is the internalization of original parental restrictions and demands. Life is a constant struggle of id versus ego and superego, and the integration of the needs of these three factions determines one's state of mental health. To the extent that one represses the instinctual needs, they create anxiety as they threaten always to break through. The individual must create "defenses" against this eventuality, but these are never more than partially successful, and the repressed urges surface in the form of neurotic symptoms or, more innocently, in dreams, slips of the tongue, or jokes.

Freud's theory of female sexuality has created a good deal of debate, especially with the recent women's movement. Freud maintained that as girls and boys become aware of their anatomical differences, girls develop envy for the sexual organ denied to them. Unfortunately, even in adulthood, a woman never gets what she seeks and never overcomes this lack. Although a woman may marry to possess the sexual organ vicariously, it is only with the birth of a male child that the woman finally feels she possesses a penis. Freud's theory of the primacy of the vaginal over clitoral orgasm related to his belief that desire for clitoral stimulation was unresolved penis envy while the ability to be satisfied through vaginal orgasm represented coming to terms with female sexuality.

The goal of Freudian therapy is to resolve the conflict between the id, ego, and superego. This is achieved when the client recognizes the existence of the instinctual urges and learns to gratify them through more socially accepted ways, such as sublimating in creative endeavors. Women are encouraged to relinquish their penis envy and accept their biologically determined passive and nurturing role in life.

The process of therapy relies heavily on free association and dream interpretation. In free association, the client is encouraged to say everything as it comes into his/her head, no matter how irrelevant or silly it seems. The client lies on a couch with the therapist out of sight. The therapist says very little so as not to interfere with the associative flow. When certain patterns become clear, the therapist will interject an interpretation. Dreams are encouraged and interpreted as distorted statements of repressed wishes. Part of the therapy is devoted to the analysis of the "transference" by which the client is seen as relating to the therapist as he/she did to early authority figures. Freudian therapists usually insist on a minimum of three sessions a week, more often four or five. Some therapists also lay down certain rules governing outside behavior, including prohibitions against talking to anyone about the therapy and making any changes in life-style during therapy. Though Freud argued against medical analysis, most Freudian therapists in this country are psychiatrists because most psychoanalytic associations, until recently, would accept only physicians for training.

Freudian therapy is a mixture of patriarchal control and partial liberation. Though the therapy is aimed at revealing unconscious drives, clients are required to sublimate rather than act on them. A passive attitude is encouraged in therapy itself by having the client lie on the couch and accept interpretations. Clients not in agreement with Freudian therapy will find themselves in fruitless struggles with the therapist about interpretations. Women especially find Freudian therapy hard to take unless they accept that true happiness lies in the path of passive nurturing and renunciation of their "masculine" strivings. Some clients find the lack of face-to-face contact with the therapist and the limited personal interaction frustrating. A lot of people, including therapists, have been drawn to Freudian therapy because it has the glitter of the "original"; and the policy of limiting membership in the American Psychoanalytic Association gave Freudian therapy an aura of some exclusivity.

Adler and Individual Psychology

Alfred Adler was the first of Freud's colleagues to split off and develop a new system. Adler was interested in the capacity of the body to compensate for organic damage. From this he developed his basic thesis that all human striving is directed toward compensating for feelings of inferiority. According to Adler, the striving for superiority and power, rather than the sexual instinct, determines human behavior. Human problems are therefore social rather than sexual in nature, with neurosis resulting when the drive to power is blocked.

As children grow they become aware of their inferiority to and dependency on adults. This "inferiority complex" can become exaggerated in many ways: by parents who are rejecting, by sibling position, or by actual "organ inferiority." A person can compensate for feelings of inferiority either by competitive achievement and gaining power over others, or by retreating from direct competition and social interaction. The individual's manner of striving for power or superiority is his/her "life-style," which is always unique. The goal of therapy is to understand this life-style and develop ways of achieving a sense of power without losing one's "community feeling."

Although Karen Horney usually gets the credit, Adler was the first disciple of Freud to develop a theory of female psychology based on woman's social role rather than on her anatomy. Women are jealous of men, according to Adler, not because of the latter's sexual organ but because men have social advantages and power.

The focus in Adlerian therapy is on understanding present life-style and future goals, rather than on the past. The therapy relationship is regarded as a model for other relationships and is aimed at developing positive feelings for other people. The therapist, in face-to-face encounters, helps the client to substitute realistic for unrealistic goals and encourages social consciousness and activism. Power strivings are unblocked and steered into socially useful channels. Adlerian therapists are directive and active, and usually see clients two times a week for several years.

Jung and Analytic Psychology

Jung, the favorite and only prominent non-Jewish student of Freud, could not accept what he considered to be Freud's excessive emphasis on sex. The system he developed was both desexualized and more esoteric and elaborate than that of his mentor.

The basic motivating force in Jungian theory is the "lifeforce," which is similar to Freud's libido but not exclusively sexual in nature. The psyche has three levels: consciousness, the personal unconscious, and the collective unconscious. The outer crust of the personality is the "persona" or façade, which is the part exposed to others. This conscious self has different ways of apprehending the world—either by introversion or by extroversion, and different functions in so doing—thinking, intuition, feeling, or sensuousness. The personal unconscious is a mirror-image of the consciousness and compensates for what is weak in the consciousness. For example, an introvert has an extroverted side of which he/she is not aware. The personal unconscious thereby contains the potential for richer functioning. The collective unconscious consists of memories inherited from earlier generations, which provide a reserve of wisdom on which consciousness can draw. Emotional problems arise from an imbalance between the various aspects of the self. The goal of therapy is to integrate those aspects of the personal unconscious that are repressed and underutilized and to bring the client into contact with the collective unconscious.

Jungian therapy focuses on present and future strivings rather than on the past. A lot of attention is given to dreams, which are considered to be a source of revelation leading to integration of the personality. The therapist takes a directive role and introjects his/her own associations to help the client progress to the point the therapist has reached. Jung felt that his therapy was most appropriate for older people past the age of forty. He thought that two times a week was adequate and that clients needed at least twenty-four hours to assimilate the materials covered in a session. While some people are drawn to Jungian therapy because of its concept of the collective unconscious and the striving for self-transcendence, others reject it for being too mystical.

Reich and Vegetotherapy

Although Reich was originally one of Freud's favored students, the two men came into conflict over Reich's radicalism. Reich was concerned with the relation of political repression to character formation, an idea that was mocked by the psychoanalytic establishment. He was also held in disfavor by political radicals for his attempts to introduce sexual reforms. After coming to the United States, Reich continued to find himself at odds with practically everyone. Events culminated in his arrest and imprisonment by federal authorities in connection with FDA curbs imposed on his marketing of therapeutic devices.

Reich felt that character is formed in order to meet the needs of the existing social order, and that individual needs have to be repressed to meet the demands of authority. Sexual needs, as the first to come into conflict with society, are the first to be suppressed. This suppression lays the groundwork for a permeating restrictive pattern running through the entire personality. Restricting the sexual impulse cripples the whole personality and it is only through sexual freedom that the individual can find personal freedom. Sexuality, as expressed in the orgasm, is the key to healthy personality functioning. The goal of therapy is to restore the motility and flow of biological energy or "orgone."

Character traits such as ambition or passivity, which form the "character armor," are developed to protect the individual from his/her instincts and constitute the roots of psychological disturbance. The character armor has a corresponding muscular armor, which is evidenced in idiosyncratic postures and movements of the body.

Therapy proceeds on both a verbal and a body-contact level, although most Reichians focus on body work. The therapist must penetrate the character armor by pointing out to the client characteristic attitudes that are used as defenses. The therapist focuses on how a person walks, sits, looks, breathes, and talks, and reads the emotions through their physical expression. The therapist also works through the layers of muscular armor, using yelling, pounding, kicking, to have the client experience the physical aspects of emotions. The client lies disrobed on a couch to make visible the areas of body tension and to make them available for manipulation that, combined with deep breathing exercises, leads to relaxation. The therapy must also work toward mature sexual functioning by helping the client achieve full orgasm.

Reichian therapy has a reputation of being "far-out." Reich's reputation as a "kook" is related to the nude body work, a concept that was far ahead of its time, and to his orgone theory and orgone-accumulating boxes. Reactions to Reichian therapy seem to be strongly positive or negative. On the positive side, people have found it helpful in putting them in touch with feelings and bodily sensations that would not emerge otherwise. Clients who have reacted negatively tend to find the therapy either too intrusive or too sexually oriented. People tend to go to Reichian therapy after becoming dissillusioned with conventional psychoanalytic approaches.

Rank and Will Therapy

Rank, another of Freud's students, was concerned with finding a briefer method of psychoanalysis and developed a system based on the observation that the physiological effects of anxiety and birth are similar. Rank believed that all psychological problems originate in the birth trauma. Birth, the original separation from the mother, produces a reservoir of anxiety, which is triggered by all subsequent experiences of separation: weaning, loss of a loved one, and so forth. The basic motivating force, the will to life and health, is blocked by the "life fear" that self-realization will result in isolation and further separation. Dependency needs and the unconscious desire to "return to the womb" stand in the way of independence and the exercise of "constructive will."

Rankian therapy is oriented to reliving the birth trauma, resolving separation anxiety, and developing the will toward autonomy. It is a short-term, intensive therapy with active therapist intervention. Although there are few Rankians to be found, elements of Rankian therapy can be found in other systems, including primal therapy. Some clients, while drawn to the therapy because of its emphasis on the development of the will, find it hard to accept the role of the birth trauma and the attempt to re-create this experience.

Horney and the Cultural Approach

Originally an orthodox Freudian analyst in Germany, Horney later became a leader of the "cultural school" of psychoanalysis in the United States. According to Horney, the search for security is the basic human drive. When the individual's security is threatened, he/she develops anxiety. To cope with these feelings of helplessness and isolation, the individual develops various strategies, which tend to differ according to the particular culture. Horney described ten coping patterns, which can be reduced to three basic strategies: moving toward people (in which the individual may accept his/her basic helplessness and look toward others for affection and support), moving against people (in which the individual acknowledges the hostility of others and fights back), or moving away from people (in which the individual just tries to keep apart). Although one strategy predominates in any individual, all are present to some degree. Some persons can create balance among the strategies, but others are unable to resolve the clash, which results in neurotic conflict. This is intensified by the inflexibility of the neurotic, who sticks to a particular strategy even though it is inappropriate. The neurotic creates an idealized self-image that denies or condemns shortcomings in the actual self and prevents the "real" self from emerging. The goal of therapy is to help the real self in each individual come to the surface. This is accomplished by facing the idealized and actual selves, and creating a balance among the three different ways of approaching the world (to, against, and away).

Horney became prominent in the 1940s and 1950s as a result of several books on therapy for the general public. Her popularity among women was especially strong: not only was she a woman but she developed a theory of female sexuality based on women's cultural role. Her break with the psychoanalytic establishment and her initiation of a rival psychoanalytic society also won her many adherents.

The therapy process is similar to Freud's, consisting of free association, interpretation, and working through. However, the therapist is more directive, focusing on fighting the prideful ideal self and on realistically facing the actual self. Therapy frequency is about three times a week, generally for a period of several years.

Sullivan and Interpersonal Relations

Sullivan was the first native American psychiatrist to develop a prominent psychoanalytic theory. Together with Horney, he broke from the ranks of the Freudians to help establish what became known as the cultural school of psychoanalysis.

People's primary strivings are, to Sullivan, the pursuit of satisfactions and the pursuit of security. Satisfactions include all physical needs; security needs are culturally determined. The environment regards the child as "good" or "bad" depending on its behavior; security comes from the approval one receives from being good, while being bad leads to disapproval and a sense of insecurity. These basic attitudes about oneself are always experienced in relation to interpersonal situations, and the self-concept is based on the perceived reactions of others. These perceptions can be accurate or they can be distorted. Once the self is developed, it maintains its form and is directed toward avoiding anxiety. People therefore tend to block out everything that threatens the way in which they have organized the self-system and that provokes anxiety. Even "hateful" self-systems are maintained by misinterpreting or ignoring friendly overtures from others.

One of the major goals of therapy is to help the client see the way in which his/her relationships are based on distorted perceptions of others. The therapy must be an interpersonal process with the therapist in the role of "participant observer." Therapy focuses on childhood experiences that have created distortions and there is a back and forth between analysis of distortions in past situations and distortions that occur between therapist and client. The relationship between therapist and client is intensified in order to release the distortions and ease resistance to change.

Because of this intensification of the therapist-client relationship, there is a potential for overly intimate involvement. In recent years, a group of Sullivanian therapists has achieved considerable notoriety with its attempts to reshape interpersonal relations by active intervention in clients' lives, including the promotion of relations within the Sullivanian community and the exclusion of others. The appeal of Sullivanian theory is thus weakened by the excesses of some of its practitioners.

Rogers and Client-Centered Therapy

The first major psychotherapy system developed by an American psychologist was Rogers's nondirective approach. The basic drive of every human being, according to Rogers, is the drive toward self-actualization. Actualization, however, can only occur in accordance with an individual's perception of him/herself. It is the perception of self that determines one's behavior and relationships with other people. Preserving and enhancing the self-concept, and obtaining positive regard from others, is a basic motivation. Experiences not consistent with one's self-concept can be disowned, and an individual may also take over values from others that are not directly experienced or are contradictory to direct experience but more congruent with the self-concept. The need to enhance the self-concept in this and other ways may come in conflict with the drive for self-actualization.

The goal in therapy is to help the client resolve this conflict by reorganizing perceptions of self and actualizing potentials for growth. The therapy process rests on providing a permissive atmosphere conducive to acquiring understanding, one in which the client's potential for constructive change is respected. The therapist tries to understand reality as experienced by the client. The client is left free to work out the course and direction of the therapeutic situation according to his/her needs. The therapist does not offer interpretations to the client but may provide summaries of material presented by the client to make sure the client is being clearly understood and to reflect back what has been said.

The major appeal of Rogerian therapy is its nonauthoritarian approach. It is better suited to clients who have the psychological resources to explore their own feelings, needing very little direction from the therapist. On the other hand, those who need more from the therapist than encouraging warmth and understanding are apt to be disappointed with this approach.

Existential Analysis

Existential analysis was developed by Ludwig Binswanger and Medard Boss, both Swiss psychiatrists. The existential therapist holds that the essence of human existence is the awareness of being. To be human is to be aware of oneself and one's world. A person exists as a "being-in-the-world" —one exists as one relates to other people and things. Human existence is the openness in which the world can disclose itself and be understood. This means that one has the responsibility to accept all the possibilities for world-disclosing relationships. Human freedom is the readiness to accept and let be all that is and can be. Human conscience is the call to fulfill the possibilities of life. People are always in debt in terms of carrying out this responsibility, since at any given moment a person can exist in only one mode of all that are possible and must leave the others unfulfilled; new possibilities are always there in the future waiting to be fulfilled. "Existential guilt" is "being-in-debt" to one's own existence.

The goal of existential therapy is to help the client understand his/her possibilities *as* possibilities and thereby permit them to unfold. The client has to acknowledge this debt to his/her own existence and accept it responsibly.

Existential analysis approaches the client without theoretical preconceptions and deals directly with what the client reveals. The focus is on understanding the immediate meaning of what the client is expressing rather than looking for what lies behind the client's behavior. The existential therapist does not ask "why" the client behaves in a certain way but rather "why not" in a more daring and less restrictive way. Therapy is not an intellectual recognition of a problem but an opportunity to experience new ways of living and relating. The therapist, by respecting and understanding the client as he/she is rather than looking for the client to confirm a theory, creates a climate in which the client feels safe enough to unfold and dare new ways of existing.

Existential analysis was introduced in the United States by Ulrich Sonnemann and Rollo May but has remained a small part of the therapy scene because it is contrary to the American predilection for systematization. Existential analysis is not interested in classifying and explaining types of behavior but in understanding and removing the restrictions that hamper a more basic engagement with the world. Though the framework is different, the procedures used in existential analysis are similar to other analytic systems: discussion, association, and dream analysis.

Gestalt Therapy

Gestalt therapy was developed by several persons, but has become most associated with Frederick S. ("Fritz") Perls. The therapy is an offshoot of Gestalt psychology, *Gestalt* being the German word for "meaningful whole."

According to Gestalt therapy, human life has a basic wholeness in which thinking, feeling, and acting are integrated. In the course of development, this unity of the self may become split. The individual also exists in the context of his environment and it is the interplay of both (figure versus ground) that provides a key to understanding. A disturbance or a lack of unified experience in the self leads to a disturbance in the figure-ground formation or the individual's relation to his/her world. An integrated person can engage freely with the world, while persons whose experiences are split tend to relate in unproductive ways. The goals of therapy are to help the individual achieve wholeness and a flexible interaction with the environment.

The therapy process is oriented toward developing awareness of, and responsiveness to, immediate experience. Emphasis is placed on the "here and now," the current experience, rather than the past or "why" of behavior. Many exercises, called "experiments in awareness," are utilized toward this end. A client may be asked to complete the statement,

"At this moment I am aware . . ." by filling in a description of what is in his/her immediate awareness. Another exercise requires the client to imagine the opposite of what he/she is wishing or experiencing. A remembering experiment instructs the client to select a recent memory and with closed eyes visualize and reconstruct the scene, noting all that is there. A body awareness exercise instructs the client to lie down and feel the body, noting aches, tension spots, uncomfortable positions, and to adjust the body smoothly. The therapist engages the client actively, directing exercises, challenging statements, rejecting certain behaviors, but also reacting sympathetically.

The awareness experiments and confrontational approach of Gestalt therapy enable many people to experience feelings that were formerly blocked. However, in the process, Gestalt therapy lends itself to intrusive and arrogant behavior on the part of therapists. For the sake of arousing feelings and developing awareness on the part of the client, some Gestalt therapists have given themselves license to behave in hostile and contemptuous ways.

Lowen and Bioenergetic Therapy

Bioenergetic therapy was developed by Alexander Lowen, an American psychiatrist who was a student of Reich. Like Reich, Lowen believes that emotional problems express themselves in the body in the form of muscular tensions, with "bioenergy," the fundamental body energy, manifesting itself on both an emotional and a muscular level. In the normal person, bodily impulses can flow to the surface, keeping the body emotionally alive and ready to respond. In others, the body is ignored and becomes a repository of repressed feelings. Therapy aims at "reclaiming" the body and enabling energy to flow freely through the organism. Since physical tensions are an expression of emotional tension, dissipating the former will help to resolve the latter.

The therapy consists of acting out emotional processes in the language of the body. Several specific exercises are employed, and clients generally wear leotards to facilitate this work. Sessions usually start with taking "stress positions" that place the muscles in a position of steady stretching. These stretch positions highlight the areas of tension and arouse bodily feelings that can be utilized during the session. Further exercises are directed toward working out inhibited reactions: a client may be asked to pound on a table while shouting "Mommy," or to grab the end of a towel held by the therapist and tug while shouting "I want it." These activities are used to develop the capacity for emotional expression, thereby increasing self-assertiveness, releasing negation, and developing affirmative feelings.

Bioenergetics appeals to people who feel they are not really at one with their physical selves and want to achieve a unity of experience. For this group, it has generally proved to be a satisfying approach. Others have found its focus too narrow to help them deal with complex problems of living.

Janov and Primal Therapy

Primal therapy was developed by Arthur Janov, an American psychologist. To Janov, the origin of emotional problems is in the daily attitudes of family life. Parents and others demand certain responses from children to fulfill their own needs, giving the child little or no opportunity for self-initiated activities and a real life. The child's primal needs for food, warmth, physical contact, and so forth are denied, resulting in primal pain. This pain accumulates, and is warded off by developing various neurotic defenses: clouded memories, reflex habits, avoiding feelings. Neurosis is a defense against primal pain.

The goal of therapy is to unearth and release the primal pain. The method used is "direct talk" to the sources of primal pain—to the authoritarian father or the overprotective mother. This direct talk goes beyond the verbal to the "primal screams" and a reexperiencing of key scenes. "Primals" are intense experiences that differ from person to person and may include screaming, writhing, sweating, trembling. Primal therapy requires three weeks of continuous individual work, usually up to three and a half hours daily, during which memories, breathing techniques, and direct verbal confrontations are utilized to bring back early experiences. Therapy is preceded by the client spending twenty-four hours in isolation indoors to deprive him/her of usual tension outlets and to weaken defenses. The therapist works with only one client for the three-week period. The client stays in therapy for up to nine months in a group setting, continuing to have cathartic experiences. Some therapists and clinics offer primal therapy on a regularly scheduled basis without the concentrated three-week period, and without total therapist availability.

Going through "primals" is emotionally demanding and not to many people's taste. There is some possibility that clients may become overwhelmed by the intensity of the experience and there is considerable question whether the release of primal pain itself is enough to be lastingly therapeutic without reintegrating uncovered feelings into the personality. Janov supports his therapy with claims of success based on physiological changes and the unabashed statement that primal therapy is *the* cure for neurosis. The dogmatism of the system and the condemnation of other approaches raises questions about the primal therapist's ability to respect clients who may be at variance with aspects of the therapy.

Transactional Analysis

Transactional Analysis was developed by Eric Berne in *Games People Play* and popularized further by Thomas Harris in *I'm OK—You're OK*. It is based on the conception that people are motivated by important social hungers as well as by biological drives. These hungers are satisfied by "stroking," which is any act that recognizes the presence of another person. The first is stimulation hunger, which is satisfied by physical stroking. Recognition hunger can be satisfied by positive strokes such as applause, smiles, kisses, or by negative strokes such as frowns or disapproval. Negative strokes, while not as satisfying as positive strokes, still afford some recognition. "Crooked" strokes are mixed messages combining both positive and negative elements. Structure hunger is the need to organize one's time, and people arrange their activities to obtain the most strokes. There are six basic ways of structuring time, going from the safest to the most exciting: withdrawal, in which the individual avoids others and satisfies him/herself with "stored" strokes, which may be relived from previous situations; rituals or stylized ways of interaction;

activities or work; pastimes; games, which are social transactions leading to a "payoff"; and, finally, intimacy, which is an open give-and-take between people. These ways of structuring time are incorporated into a larger structure called the life plan or "script," which is developed in childhood.

Each individual has three aspects of personality: the Child (impulse aspect), the Parent (critical aspect), and the Adult (mature aspect). A stable person can change from one state to another depending on its appropriateness to the situation, but others may be stuck in a particular state or have one state contaminated by another. In social transactions, people can communicate satisfactorily only when these states are complementary to one another. When the states are crossed, for instance one person's Child talking to another person's Adult, this leads to conflict. Most transactions are complex and ulterior, with more than two states activated at the same time, one covering up the other. Ulterior transactions are the basis for games, which always involve a con.

The goal of therapy is to help the client move from games to intimacy and to avoid self-destructive scripts. The methods of Transactional Analysis consist of "structural analysis" in which the interaction of the three states of the client are analyzed, and in analyzing scripts. Therapy can be individual, but is usually conducted on a group basis because the latter provides greater opportunity for analyzing transactions. The therapist is active and direct in pointing out the three different states in which clients are interacting, in diagnosing their games and scripts, and in convincing clients that they need not be victims of these problems.

Transactional Analysis has appeal because it is relatively easy to understand, not very demanding of the client, and supportive in unraveling difficulties in interpersonal relationships. However, in its focus on interpersonal behavior, Transactional Analysis often bypasses the inner person.

Ellis and Rational-Emotive Therapy

Rational-emotive therapy was developed by Albert Ellis, an American psychologist. The therapy is based on the view that emotions are a form of evaluative thought. Positive emotions result from experiences labeled as "good" and negative emotions are caused by the label of "bad." Controlling one's emotions is accomplished by controlling one's thoughts. Emotions can be changed from negative to positive by reevaluating or relabeling situations. Emotional disturbances result from repeating to oneself negative and illogical thoughts. The individual develops these thoughts in relation to the environment. Parents and the larger culture provide many damaging evaluations and irrational beliefs, which are then internalized.

The goal of therapy is to show the client the nature of these irrational beliefs and induce him/her to adopt more rational ideas. To achieve these goals, the therapist takes an active and persuasive role.

Ellis feels his system is most appropriate for intelligent younger people who are not very disturbed and who are willing to work and discipline themselves. Some clients welcome the directness and firm opinionated stand of the therapist, but others find it not very conducive to reflection or to getting in touch with one's own feelings.

Family Therapy

In family therapy the focus is on bringing about changes in family relationships rather than in individuals. If it is just a husband and wife relationship, it is called marital therapy; if an unmarried relationship, it is called couples therapy.

Family therapy encompasses all the theories and methods of individual and group therapy, ranging from the psychoanalytic approach of analyzing unconscious conflicts that disturb family relationships to behavior modification aimed at changing behavior in the family by realigning reward and punishment systems. The approaches vary in the emphasis each gives to defining the causes of the problem, improving communications, finding better ways of coping with disagreement and other forms of stress, involvement of children in the process, and attention given to the needs of individual family members. Many therapists are eclectic and use whatever approach seems to get the best results with a given family.

Family therapy tends to be pragmatic, focusing on tangible results in improving family relationships. Therapists usually take a prominent role and often directly engage in family interactions. Family therapy has been innovative in developing techniques for which it has created a jargon all its own. Conjoint family therapy means that the therapy sessions include most or all of the family members. When the sessions are expanded to include other people important to the family, like neighbors, friends, or employers, it is called network family therapy. When several families meet as a group, it is called multiple family therapy. When a whole team of professionals meets with the family to provide a concentrated therapeutic impact, it is called multiple impact therapy. The last is one of several crisis intervention techniques that concern themselves with giving immediate aid in order to prevent serious family breakdowns. One form of family therapy deliberately induces crises to give the therapist opportunities for helping the family work out better ways of solving problems.

Most therapists see families on a weekly basis. The duration of therapy ranges from a few weeks to several years; on average, it lasts about one year. Family therapy may be used exclusively or as a supplementary technique.

Family therapy has become a well-established entity. Founded on the recognition that the interpersonal environment, especially the immediate family, has a crucial influence on people's psychological well-being, it developed at a time when satisfying family relationships became increasingly difficult to maintain. If the focus of emotional difficulties seems to be in these relationships, family therapy could well be the preferred approach. However, in family therapy the goal is to maintain the family unit (in marital therapy, it is the marital relationship). If an individual is not genuinely committed to that goal and secretly wants "out," but agrees to therapy because of guilt, such therapy may not serve his/her best interests. More often than not, individuals are confused and unsure of their motives. Under these circumstances, therapy that aims at discovering or actualizing individual goals is more appropriate.

Child Therapy
Psychotherapy, in the usual sense, cannot be used with young children. Exploration of one's feelings and attitudes

requires a degree of conceptual development beyond the scope of the younger child. Furthermore, children are often too intimidated by adults to talk about their feelings. This fear is intensified when children are brought to therapy by parents because of some "complaint" about them. The child then sees the therapist as an agent of the parents rather than as an ally and source of support.

Play therapy was developed as a way to overcome these obstacles. It offers children a natural medium through which they can express themselves and work out troubling feelings. Through the use of games, dolls, drawing, or by just being together, the child can give vent to painful emotions. Feelings of rejection by the family, jealousy of siblings, anger toward the parents, may all come to the fore. Acting out conflicts and reliving frightening situations through play helps the child to assimilate these experiences into his/her personality. It also helps the child attain some understanding of these difficult feelings and offers an opportunity to experiment with more appropriate ways of expressing them. Older children can engage in the more usual type of psychotherapy when they are able to talk about their problems.

Therapy with children, when limited to the child, is a partial solution. Just as with adults, the problems experienced by children arise from the situation in which they live and their interactions with others. Unlike adults, however, children have very little control over others and cannot shape their own worlds. If a child has difficulty expressing anger to his/her parents, chances are it is because the parents do not want to hear it. Enabling a child to unburden him/herself of angry feelings will have only a limited benefit if he/she has to continue living with parents who will not tolerate any expression of anger. A child with emotional problems does not have the wherewithal to resolve these problems without the active participation of the parents. Therefore it is important that the child's parents work with the therapist as well.

Child therapy is practiced by therapists using many different psychotherapy systems. More important than theoretical orientation is the therapist's ability to work with a child at the child's own level of self-expression and to incorporate the parents into the therapy. The therapist who does not work with the parents will most likely not be able to offer help of lasting benefit to the child. Child therapists vary in their attitudes about working with parents. Some encourage it, others prohibit it. Those who discourage it see parent contact as inimical to establishing a trusting relationship with the child. This attitude implicitly defines the parents as the common enemy and further alienates child and parent. It is also easier for the therapist because he/she does not have to deal with the parents. Yet, the child's fears that confidentiality may be destroyed by therapist-parent contact are allayed by having such contacts in the presence of the child. Occasional family sessions are, in any event, a preferred mode of therapy for children since the focus of the emotional problems usually lies in the family interaction.

Group Therapy

Group therapy, although practiced in many different forms, is essentially individual-centered therapy within a group situation. All major psychotherapy systems have adapted their methods of individual therapy to group use since a group setting has several advantages that individual therapy cannot provide.

Group therapy offers a ready-made circle of people who are willing to try to understand, accept, and share feelings with each other. It is especially sensitive to interpersonal difficulties since these are readily revealed in the group interaction. Uninhibited interactions are encouraged and, when achieved, inevitably lead to emotionally arousing confrontations. As a "living laboratory," groups focus on helping participants to perceive their habitual ways of dealing with interpersonal stress and to try out new ways.

While providing a greater range of stimulation, group therapy also offers greater opportunities for response. The participants have to cope with the reactions of others and can give as well as receive help. Group participation facilitates transfer of newly learned behavior into daily life.

Though there must be mutuality of purpose for group cohesion to develop, groups can be heterogeneous or homogeneous in such member characteristics as age, sex, or psychological problem area. Heterogeneous groups offer a wider range of stimulation and are intended to function as a microcosm of the larger world, while homogeneous groups (couples, divorcées, adolescents) facilitate sharing of common experiences. Therapy groups usually consist of from six to ten people and meet weekly for an hour and a half. Some groups continue for as long as group interest persists; others have a predetermined time when they will end. Most groups meet with one therapist, some with two, and some occasionally without the therapist. When two therapists are present, they are usually one of each sex to provide both "mother" and "father" figures.

Therapists vary greatly in the role they take in the group, depending on their theoretical approach and personality predispositions. Some remain neutral arbiters, some actively promote group interaction, and some become group participants. The therapist's main responsibility is to ensure that a therapeutic atmosphere is maintained and that painful experiences are utilized constructively. The influence of the group is very strong and can have important positive or negative effects. It can support a member through a critical moment in the therapy and it can foster conformity by pressuring people to participate when they want to be aloof or to accept feedback when they want to reject it.

Compared to individual therapy, group therapy provides a greater diversity of stimulation, greater opportunity to try out new ways of relating, and more time in therapy for less cost. On the other hand, group therapy offers less time for individual problems, particularly those that do not relate to interactions with others, and it provides little opportunity for examining personal experiences or for reflecting on new experiences. For that reason group therapy is frequently combined with individual therapy, although it can be and often is used by itself.

Encounter Groups

The purpose of encounter groups is to provide intense emotional experience through encounters with others. Encounter groups aim at openness of communication and stripping of façades so that people come to know one another as they really are. This permits trusting relationships that enable individual growth. Encounter groups are intended to offer intimacy as an antidote to isolation, a therapeutic "experience" rather than psychotherapy. In many ways the encounter movement represents a rebellion against conventional psychotherapy: psychotherapy systems, methods, and training are considered irrelevant to people's basic need for deeply experienced relationships with others.

With the founding of Esalen Institute, a "growth resort" at Big Sur, California, encounter groups became part of the pop culture and started mushrooming all over the country. This explosion was triggered in large part by the appeal of the psychological "turn on" encounter groups offered and their ability to satisfy people's hunger for closeness and relationships. But, more importantly, this was the first therapeutic-growth system that was widely promoted. Esalen was a major step into an organizational big-business approach to therapy.

Encounter groups consist of ten to fifteen people who meet for several sessions within a short period of time, ranging from several days to several weeks. Marathons are a form of encounter group, staying in session continuously for anywhere from the better part of a day to a weekend. A variety of verbal and nonverbal techniques (confrontation, massage, hugging) and structured exercises (telling the person next to you what you think of him/her, clapping at different rhythms, "trust" falling—falling backward into another's arms) are used to encourage uninhibited interaction among group members. Encounter groups stress the expression of feeling and bodily awareness and enjoyment; they play down intellectual understanding.

Encounter groups are now on the wane, being overtaken by new group movements such as Arica and *est.* Evaluative studies have shown little evidence of lasting therapeutic benefit and considerable evidence that they can be harmful. While most group leaders agree that seriously disturbed people should not be in encounter groups, little or no attempt is made to screen participants beforehand, nor is there any follow-up after the group sessions. The encounter group's lack of permanence works against experiencing genuine trust and intimacy, avowed to be a primary goal. Group leaders disclaim any responsibility for what happens to the participants, who are considered to be totally responsible for themselves both in and out of sessions. Encounter groups have been satisfying for people without serious problems who welcome interesting experiences that stimulate emotional growth, but they have been a disappointment for people who sought them out as a substitute for on-going psychotherapy.

est

   est is the latest rage in packaged approaches to self-realization. Founded in the 1970s by an American salesman who renamed himself Werner Erhard, Erhard Seminars Training centers on communicating the message that each person is responsible for his/her own life. The *est* program takes two consecutive weekends during which a group of approximately 250 people are led together, in a large room, through a variety of experiences by a trainer. These experiences consist of many techniques borrowed from Esalen, Gestalt, Dale Carnegie, Zen, and other movements, but put together in a structured format. Unlike the more indulgent atmosphere at Esalen, *est* is austere and Spartan, with physical discomfort as an integral part of the program. Participants sit for long hours on hard chairs with minimal breaks for food or bathroom. During the course of the session the message is constantly repeated, sometimes in rather derogatory fashion, that each participant is the cause of his/her own experience and responsible for everything that has happened.

   Run like a large business organization, *est* reportedly grossed over $9 million in 1975. It has attracted many dedicated volunteers who claim that *est* has changed their lives and who help the paid staff spread the message. Others, however, have found the seminars to be a naïve assortment of borrowed techniques with nothing new to offer. The popularity and appeal of *est* is undoubtedly related to its well-organized marketing approach and the coverage it has received in the media. Its promise of a sixty-hour transformation seems to be the panacea people have been searching for. A good number of *est* enthusiasts feel it has changed their whole approach to life, and others, although less enthusiastic, credit *est* with helping them to experience themselves more fully. But while many people have found help in coming to grips with their problems by accepting the message, most people's problems are not amenable to such a simplistic approach. Readiness to accept responsibility must be followed up by the hard and slow process of doing so. A more disturbing aspect of *est* is the worshipful attitude trainers and converts hold toward Erhard. Any system that thrives on such adoration of the leader does not seem consonant with the development of positive attitudes about one's self.

Hypnotherapy

Hypnotherapy is the application of hypnosis to alleviate psychological distress and problems. According to one of its major proponents, hypnosis by itself has no permanent psychotherapeutic effects but it can be of specific benefit in conjunction with psychotherapy. Hypnosis has been used to remove temporarily such incapacitating hysterical symptoms as paralysis, tics, and amnesia. While relieved of such symptoms, a client may be able to work psychotherapeutically to get at the causes of the symptoms. Hypnosis is also used to reduce resistance and to help bring repressed memories to the surface. Some hypnotherapists use it as a form of persuasion, trying to have the client accept attitudes and values in a trance state that are being resisted in a waking state. Hypnosis has also been used as a way to break undesirable habits such as smoking and overeating.

Hypnotherapy is limited in application to persons who are suggestible and can be hypnotized to the necessary depth. Hypnotic suggestions have a limited life-span and unless the problems a symptom is expressing are worked through in a waking state, the symptom is apt to reappear. Similarly, repressed material that emerges in a trance is helpful only to the extent that it can be integrated into one's waking state and consciousness.

Hypnotherapy is potentially detrimental in that the client yields control of him/herself to an outside authority. Aside from the long-range implications of such a renunciation of self-responsibility, it very clearly makes the client dependent on the good graces of the hypnotherapist.

Behavior Therapy/Behavior Modification

Although behavior therapy is often considered to be a form of psychotherapy, it is a system apart because it is exclusively concerned with changing behavior and not with increasing awareness. What the psychotherapist sees as emotional problems to be clarified, the behavior modifier sees as maladaptive habits to be changed. Behavior therapy asserts that all behavior is a learned response to the environment. The goal of behavior modification is to extinguish old maladaptive responses and to elicit new responses. Its methods are based on the principles of learning theory, which hold that people persist in behavior that is rewarded and desist from behavior that is punished. By punishing negative responses and reinforcing positive responses, the individual is conditioned to respond in new ways. This is done in two steps. First, the behavior therapist conducts a behavioral analysis, which is a study of events leading up to and following a particular unwanted behavior. Next, the therapist designs and carries out a program of treatment to modify that behavior.

Several techniques have been developed to modify behavior. "Systematic desensitization" is used to reduce the anxiety associated with a certain situation and thereby eliminate avoidance of the feared situation. Fear of snakes, or of riding in elevators, are examples of maladaptive behaviors that are treated by systematic desensitization. Treatment involves exposure by progressive steps to the feared situations. The client's fears are ordered from the least to the greatest, and he/she is exposed to them one by one. This is done either by imagining the feared situations or by actual exposure. Fear of snakes might be treated by first talking about snakes, then looking at snake pictures, then looking at live snakes, touching a live snake held by someone else, and finally by handling a live snake oneself. Each new step is undertaken only after fear at the previous step is dissipated.

"Operant conditioning" is used in conditions that require complex behavior change, such as school failure or stuttering. Operant conditioning is based on the premise that behavior is affected by its consequences. It changes conditions in the environment that reward unwanted behavior and introduces positive reinforcement for desired behavior. "Token economies," a form of operant conditioning, are used to reward positive behavior. When the client makes a desired response, he/she receives a token that can be exchanged later for some direct reward. For example, a child who wets the bed may be given a gold star each night he/she stays dry; after getting seven stars in a row, they may be traded in for a toy.

"Aversion therapy" involves punishing the undesired behavior in order to extinguish it. For example, a transvestite is asked to dress in women's clothes while in the therapist's office. While doing so he is given electric shocks until the clothes are entirely removed. This procedure is repeated during office visits until the client finally refuses to wear women's clothes outside as well as inside the therapist's office.

Behavior modification has generated much controversy not because of how well it does or does not work but because of its broader implications. Behavior therapy, like medical treatment, focuses on the symptoms and seeks to remove them without regard to their meaning for the individual. It holds that relief from the symptom is sufficient in and of itself and that the ends justify the means. It ignores what the symptom is trying to communicate and bypasses the inner turmoil it expresses. Behavior modification is a "law and order" approach to the individual, seeking socially adaptive behavior rather than expanded horizons. It encourages the individual to look for control rather than to exercise self-control. The acceptance of deliberate control of human behavior dehumanizes the individual and is the essence of totalitarianism. While behavior modifiers contend that the client retains responsibility because he/she decides which behavior patterns will be modified, the process requires the individual to relinquish responsibility for him/herself.

Behavior therapy has been successful in treating specific behavioral problems such as phobias, sexual deviancy, and enuresis, but it has had little effect on complex emotional problems. Because such problems are beyond the scope of behavior modification, behavior modifiers are turning back to a consideration of the processes that go on within a person. To the extent that they do, they can be more successful in helping people come to terms with their problems, but to the same extent they are no longer doing behavior therapy. Many psychotherapists incorporate behavior modification techniques into the psychotherapy process. When used as an adjunct to psychotherapy, these techniques can facilitate therapy by relieving anxieties and other symptoms and leaving clients freer to focus on underlying problems. They can be and often are used informally to encourage a client to exercise new capabilities. The critical difference between the supplementary use of behavior modification techniques in psychotherapy and their exclusive use is the difference between changing one's life and changing one's habits.

Sex Therapy

Sex therapy is a form of behavior modification that concentrates on sexual problems such as premature ejaculation, impotence, and orgasmic dysfunction. The usual procedure is for clients to work in pairs. Clients who are engaged in a sexual relationship, marital or otherwise, come with their partner. Other clients, depending on the clinic, may be provided with a partner by the clinic.

The couple works with two therapists, one male and one female. Although there is variation in procedure, a common pattern is for the couple to engage in an intensive two-week treatment period during which they are seen daily. The therapy is a reconditioning process aimed at reducing performance fears. Through a series of graduated homework assignments, the couple goes on to different levels of sexual activity, moving on to a new level only once comfort and satisfaction have been achieved at the previous level.

Sex therapy has had some degree of success, primarily where the sexual problem was grounded in a lack of information, in misinformation, in lack of technical know-how, or in reluctance to deal with associated anxiety. Where the sexual problems have been expressions of deep-seated emotional attitudes and the sex therapy has isolated sexual behavior from the feelings involved toward the sexual partner and toward oneself, it has not been very successful. Impotency, for example, could reflect various attitudes: it could be a statement of feelings of guilt in having sex and the expectation of punishment; it could be a statement of general feelings of incompetence and powerlessness; it could be a statement of feelings about the sexual partner as being undeserving; or it could be a way of getting back at one's partner. Masters and Johnson, probably the best-known proponents of sex therapy, have given recognition to this omission, including in their latest work on sex a discussion of the importance of feelings and attitudes toward one's partner. However, it should be borne in mind that when sex therapy does explore feelings and attitudes, it is introducing psychotherapy techniques even though remaining basically symptom oriented.

The field of sex therapy has become one of grave abuse and commercial exploitation. In considering sex therapy, utmost care must be used in checking on the credentials and reputation of the therapist. Many so-called sex clinics are but thinly disguised procurement agencies.

Medical Treatment

Medical treatment is by far the most commonly used technique other than psychotherapy for alleviating psychological discomfort. It is also the most abused and dangerous technique.

Since the body and the mind are not separate entities but together constitute the person, it is reasonable to assume that psychological problems influence body functioning just as bodily processes influence psychological states. Recent research has provided evidence that imbalances in the body's chemistry are correlated with the more severe psychological disturbances such as schizophrenia and manic-depressive psychosis. However, just as with the chicken and the egg, we do not know which causes what. Nonetheless, the medical approach assumes that psychological problems, which are called "mental illnesses," are just like bodily illnesses and require medical treatment. This approach ignores that most psychological problems do not have a physiological base and that even those that are interrelated cannot be "cured" merely by the administration of medical treatment without regard for the whole person. Since so little is known about the underlying physiological conditions of psychological stress, most medical treatment is limited to alleviating symptoms. Those psychiatrists who are concerned with curing basic biochemical imbalances related to psychological problems rather than treating the symptoms of such imbalance are a minuscule group derided by organized medicine.

The widespread use of medical treatment for psychological conditions can be traced to several factors. The predominant one is professional self-interest: it is a convenient and profitable treatment to administer. But it has subjected the public to many abuses, including unnecessary, irrelevant, and harmful treatment, as well as excessive costs. Fortunately, some members of the psychiatric profession, including Thomas Szasz and Eileen Walkenstein, are now speaking out against these abuses and trying to alert people to the dangers. The public has been willing to accept medical treatment for psychological problems because it is in awe of the medical profession. Many people also find medical treatment attractive because it reduces the symptoms accompanying emotional problems. A person can get quick relief from insomnia or anxiety by taking pills. The trouble is that the convenience comes at a high price. When treatment is discontinued the symptoms usually reappear. Addiction and overdose more commonly result from the use of prescribed drugs than from the use of illegal drugs, and the more effective drugs are those with more dangerous side effects. These associated physiological problems are only part of the cost; palliative medical treatment also means that the person is diverted from his/her real problems. When the symptoms are reduced, one loses the motivation to deal with the causes of the difficulty. By dulling the senses, one becomes less aware of what is going on in oneself rather than becoming more aware and more in tune with the world.

Some psychiatrists, in recognizing the drawbacks of medical treatment, use it only as a means of making patients more receptive to the psychotherapy process. Drugs or megavitamins can be used to reduce excessive anxiety or other symptoms so that serious psychotherapeutic work becomes possible. Under these circumstances, medical treatment can be a useful adjunct to psychotherapy.

There are several important things to keep in mind if you are considering medical treatment.

- Do not consent to such treatment just because a psychiatrist or physician tells you it is necessary. The decision to accept medical treatment is yours, and you should agree only if it makes sense to you. It is a good idea to obtain a second opinion before consenting to treatment consisting of anything more than temporary administration of mild tranquilizers or megavitamins.

Many psychiatrists want you to take medication because they are uncomfortable with your anxiety, but you should take medication only when *you* cannot deal with it.

- Do not accept medical treatment if it is not prescribed in conjunction with a medical checkup and history. The prescribing physician should be aware of any medical problems, allergies, or drug reactions you have, as well as any other medications you are taking. When in psychotherapy, whether with a psychiatrist or nonmedical therapist, it may be preferable to obtain medication, if necessary, from your regular physician. That person will be able to prescribe more safely having a better knowledge of your bodily functioning.

- Do not accept any treatment before finding out possible side effects. People are increasingly and properly concerned about the harmful effects of taking drugs or undergoing other treatment. Physicians tend to take the attitude that side effects are statistically improbable, and that the results are worth the risk. Since the decision concerns you and your body, you are the one to determine how much risk you want to take. You may not feel that medication has been in your best interest if you happen to fall into that small percentage of cases that develops adverse reactions.

There are four basic categories of medical treatment, as follows:

Psychoactive Drugs Psychoactive or mood-altering drugs have become as much a part of the American scene as the hamburger, and they have been marketed just as aggressively by the drug companies. Yet, despite their acceptance as part of daily life, they are potentially dangerous drugs. The psychoactive drugs fall into several broad categories. The minor tranquilizers or sedatives (the best-known brands being Valium and Librium) can be helpful in reducing anxiety. Their side effects include drowsiness, lethargy, and withdrawal reactions after large doses. They should not be used in conjunction with alcohol, or with a variety of other drugs. These drugs can lead to habituation and dependency.

The major tranquilizers or antipsychotic drugs are used

to calm overexcitement and hyperactivity and to reduce such symptoms as anxiety, thought disturbance, and withdrawal. The most popular brand names are Stelazine, Thorazine, and Mellaril. Dangerous side effects, including faintness, palpitation, and involuntary muscle movements similar to those of Parkinson's disease, may occur even from small doses of these drugs. Extreme caution must be used in prescribing them and they should be considered only for severe disturbances and if milder medications have been unsuccessful. They are often prescribed in conjunction with other drugs that can counteract some of the side effects, but the counteractive drugs can produce side effects of their own.

The antidepressants form another category of drugs and, in turn, break down into three subgroups. The tricyclics (Elavil and Tofranil among others) and the MAO inhibitors (Marplan, Parnate, Nardil) are effective in relieving simple depression but they should not be used in combination with each other or when there are signs of cardiovascular disease or high blood pressure. They can take weeks or months to have effect. The MAO inhibitors are also dangerous to use in conjunction with various foods including cheese, chocolate, and certain fish. Adverse side effects from both groups include constipation, urinary retention, and dryness of mouth. In addition, tricyclics can cause palpitations, tremors, excess sweating, and blurred vision, while the MAO inhibitors can cause dizziness, loss of appetite, inhibition of ejaculation, and jaundice. The third group is the amphetamines or "speed" (including Benzedrine and Dexedrine), which are prescribed for narcolepsy, for children diagnosed as having minimal brain dysfunction, and for adult weight reduction. The amphetamines can be habit forming and should not be used for long periods of time. They should also not be used if there is any indication of heart disease or high blood pressure. Adverse side effects include insomnia, restlessness, palpitations, and dependence. When abused they can produce bizarre symptoms including extreme aggressiveness and thought disorders.

Another drug family, derived from lithium carbonate, is frequently characterized as antidepressant but is intended only for blocking the manic phase of manic-depressive disorders. Because of its sudden popularity it is now being promoted for other forms of depression as well. Lithium's side effects include fatigue, slurred speech, muscle weakness, unsteady gait, tremors, nausea, vomiting, and diarrhea, and it should not be used by persons on a salt-free diet. Popular brand names are Lithane and Lithonate.

A frequently prescribed drug not falling into any of the above categories is Ritalin, which is used primarily for treatment of minimal brain dysfunction in children. It should not be used in cases of marked anxiety, or agitation, in the presence of seizures, or for children under six. Side reactions include insomnia, nervousness, loss of appetite, nausea, palpitations, headache. Ritalin may cause drug dependency.

Electric Shock   While originally administered only in hospital settings, electric shock treatment has spread to private psychiatric practice. It consists of the induction of an electric current through the brain, causing convulsion and coma. It is usually administered in series of six to ten treatments, which may then be repeated. Electric shock is mainly useful in the treatment of depression but it is also used for some schizophrenic reactions. Although electric shock can wipe out some symptoms temporarily it is a dangerous technique that can result in lasting memory loss and, perhaps, irreversible damage to the brain. Electric shock is a handy form of therapy for unscrupulous psychiatrists. Using this technique, they can handle a large number of patients who are charged $50 to $75 and more for each treatment, which lasts only minutes. Psychiatric offices specializing in this technique are known as "shock mills." While many psychiatrists consider electric shock to be an "efficient" way to treat symptoms, its dangers are too great for you to submit willingly to such treatment.

Psychosurgery   In psychosurgery parts of the brain are destroyed to alter a person's behavior; it is used mostly to control aggressive behavior. Psychosurgery is the most hazardous form of medical treatment because the effects are irreversible. Afterward, a person can never be the same again. Psychosurgery generally leads to apathy, mental impairment, a blunting of the personality, and sometimes to convulsive seizures. Though psychosurgery gained a modicum of public support as a treatment of last resort for chronic psychiatric patients, the technique has been used experimentally with a much wider range of patients. It has even been used on children to reduce hyperactivity. Some attempts to control such unwarranted use of psychosurgery are now under way. If psychosurgery can be legally defined as an experimental process, it will provide much-needed public safeguards and protect people from involuntary surgery for behavior control.

Orthomolecular Psychiatry   Recognizing the possibility of a biochemical basis to some emotional disturbances, orthomolecular therapy is oriented to restoring the proper biochemical balance with various nutrients. The therapy consists of diet control, usually through the elimination of sugars and starches and by taking megadoses of various vitamins (primarily B's, C, and E) and trace elements (primarily zinc). The typical American diet is conspicuously lacking in B vitamins and very high in sugars, which destroy the limited B's in today's processed foods. Dietary deficiencies, as, for example, in scurvy conditions, are known to create psychological disturbances that disappear when the deficiencies are corrected.

While orthomolecular psychiatrists are greeted with derision by the medical profession, they have reported dramatic results with many patients. Orthomolecular therapy has been particularly effective with children diagnosed as hyperactive or as having minimal brain dysfunction. Orthodox psychiatric treatment puts such children on a program of amphetamines or Ritalin to reduce the symptoms. Dr. Benjamin Feingold, whose work in this area is most widely known, has found that many of these symptoms disappear by eliminating from a child's diet all foods containing chemical additives, such as colorants and flavorings, and by introducing essential foods that might be lacking. Many so-called problem children have become "normal" once given a sound diet.

Since few health practitioners in this country are informed about nutrition or care much about it, it is difficult to find someone who will be willing to work with you or your child in this way. Nevertheless it would seem to be a safe alternative to try with anybody whose diet suggests biochemical imbalance and whose psychological problem has proven amenable to such treatment in others, for example, hyperactivity, general irritability, and learning disability.

3.
How to Pick a Therapist

THE COMPETENCE OF THE THERAPIST AND HIS/HER compatability with the client are the most important factors determining the outcome of psychotherapy. Yet most people entering psychotherapy never really choose a therapist, but take the first name they get. They are afraid to "shop around" because they feel intimidated and unsure of what to look for. But it is possible to choose a therapist and to pick a person who is suitable for you. If there is a lack of choice in your locale, you might want to travel farther to get the right therapist rather than settle for whomever is close at hand. In looking for a therapist, remind yourself that you are buying a service, that you are a client to be satisfied, that you have a right to ask questions about the service you are buying. The more particular you are in your choice, the better your chances for good psychotherapy.

What to Look For
Your therapist should be a person with the particular knowledge, skills, and personal characteristics necessary to conduct psychotherapy. Specifically, the therapist should be educated in personality theory, be experienced in conducting psychotherapy, have had personal psychotherapy, and be a wholesome, sensitive person who respects others.
While these requirements might seem obvious, they cannot be taken for granted just because a person hangs out a shingle. Unfortunately, the diplomas on the wall or the string of degrees after the name do not necessarily tell you

whether a potential therapist meets these basic requirements. These are matters you are going to have to investigate for yourself, in ways to be discussed.

Professional Orientations

Since there is no primary profession of psychotherapy, psychotherapists enter the field from one of several related disciplines. Medicine, psychology, and social work are the most prominent, but recently nursing has also become a professional route to psychotherapy.

Each profession approaches people and their psychological problems from a different perspective: medicine (and nursing) through the body, psychology through the personality, and social work through the society.

Medicine and its subspecialty psychiatry see emotional problems as a form of illness to be treated like other diseases. Psychiatry thereby falls prey to using technologically oriented medical treatment for psychological conditions. Medication, electric-shock therapy, and psychosurgery are the natural consequences of this orientation. While some emotional disturbances can be alleviated by medical treatment, that is not psychotherapy. Unfortunately, many psychiatrists are not clear on the difference and consider a ten-minute session in which medication schedules are checked as "psychotherapy."

As Freud first suggested, medicine and psychotherapy are basically incompatible. In the medical approach, the individual becomes a "patient" to be treated, not a person to be engaged in an active psychotherapy process that stimulates growth. It stands to reason that psychiatrists call persons to whom they render psychotherapy "patients" while therapists from other professions, although generally adopting this custom, sometimes call them "clients." The medical approach requires the "patient" to relinquish authority and let the physician take over.

Another difficulty inherent in the medical approach is that physicians are trained to focus on the disease rather than on the individual in order to retain "objectivity" and stay personally uninvolved. But psychotherapy as an interpersonal process requires the therapist's active engagement with the client, and the psychiatrist must therefore learn to drop his/her shield to relate in a personal way.

Of course, many psychiatrists overcome these medical attitudes as they practice psychotherapy. Indeed, the most prominent advocates of genuine psychotherapy have been psychiatrists, and members of that profession have been in the forefront in developing new theories and approaches in psychotherapy. Practically every psychotherapy system has been originated by a psychiatrist.

Psychology's route to understanding emotional problems is through a study of the personality. Among all the professions, it is the most directly related to psychotherapy since its subject matter is psychological processes.

Clinical psychology has taken two major roads. On the one hand, psychology can be credited with the development of the humanist–existential–client-centered approaches that are oriented toward enabling people to reach their potential and recover responsibility for their own existence. These approaches have helped to dispel the archaic and dangerous notions implicit in the mental illness concept, while also restoring dignity to the person with emotional problems.

On the other hand, psychology is largely responsible for the development of behavior modification. This technique grew out of the belief that observable behavior, rather than underlying motivations, is the proper area of concern for psychology. Here, the "unconscious" and other inner mental processes are regarded as unscientific entities not worthy of study. Behavior modification adopts an overly simplistic, mechanistic view of people, ignores individual responsibility for behavior, and puts control for personal development in the hands of another. This outgrowth of psychology is as incompatible with psychotherapy as is the medical model.

Social work tries to understand human problems through their relationship to society. The field has, as its primary focus, making social services available to those in need. The bias from which social workers must free themselves in order to practice psychotherapy is that of helping the client by direct intervention rather than through working toward changes that emerge from the client. Social work has also been more concerned with the individual as he/she relates to others and the emphasis in psychotherapy is therefore apt to be on interpersonal processes rather than on intrapsychic difficulties. The major contribution of social work to psychotherapy has been in the application of family therapy and other therapy forms that work with interpersonal networks rather than individuals.

Nursing has entered the field of psychotherapy too recently to discern any clear trends. Since nursing is part of medicine, a psychotherapist who chooses to train in that field has to overcome an initial bias toward viewing emotional problems as mental illness and must also become comfortable in the role of independent practitioner.

Related to these differences in orientation are differences among the practitioners in the major professions in terms of motives for entering the field, affiliations, and attitudes toward each other.* Psychiatrists tend to enter the field because of parental influence and the desire to gain identity and professional status. Psychologists are more influenced by teachers and the intellectual stimulation provided by psychotherapy and enter the field because of a desire to understand people. Social workers are influenced by co-professionals and enter the field out of a desire to help people. Most psychotherapists have other work in addition to private practice: psychiatrists work more frequently in hospital settings, psychologists as academicians, and social workers in clinical or social agencies. Of all the professions, psychiatrists have a higher proportion of political conservatives, with the more conservative being more prone to administer drugs and shock. There is much rivalry among the professions, especially between psychiatrists and psychologists, which colors the images and attitudes the three professions have toward each other. The psychiatrists are seen as having an authoritarian and rigid personality with a godlike complex. Psychologists are seen as intellectual and conceptual and as aggressive and competitive. Social workers are seen as dedicated people concerned with helping others.

Education and Training

The training offered by these professions varies substantially in how close it comes to meeting the basic requisites for

* For the actual researches that support the observations that follow, see the suggested reading list at the end of this book.

psychotherapists. None is adequate by itself. Therefore, responsible therapists supplement their preparation with specialized training in psychotherapy. Usually such training is obtained through postgraduate psychotherapy training institutes, most of which only accept candidates with a doctoral degree (PhD or MD) although some accept candidates below this level. They offer a certificate in psychotherapy based on the completion of theoretical course work in personality and psychotherapy, a specified number of hours providing psychotherapy under supervision, and personal psychotherapy.

A description of the training given by medicine, psychology, and social work shows what is provided and what is left out, which credentials are relevant and which are not. Examining the assumptions implicit in the training will also help you evaluate the compatibility of the different professional backgrounds to your needs in psychotherapy.

Medicine The training of psychiatrists is basically in medicine. It consists of four years in medical school leading to an MD degree and one year in an internship. Since psychiatry is a branch of medicine, to practice psychiatry one must have a medical license, but beyond this the title "psychiatrist" is not controlled and no approval from an accrediting body is necessary to assume that title.

After the basic medical degree, most psychiatrists go through a three-year residency training program in psychiatry. Until recently, many residencies were limited to medical treatment of chronic hospitalized patients and provided little or no experience in psychotherapy. Lately, there has been greater emphasis on teaching psychotherapy skills in residency programs.

About one-third of all psychiatrists are board certified. Certification is awarded by the American Board of Psychiatry and Neurology if the psychiatrist has passed special examinations that he/she is eligible to take after three years of residency and two additional years of practice. Some psychiatrists were awarded their certificate without this examination under the "grandfather clause" because they were in practice prior to the initiation of the board. However, since the board examinations focus on psychiatric issues such as diagnosis and medication rather than on psychotherapy skills, board certification does not necessarily indicate competence in psychotherapy.

The psychiatrist who wants to obtain specialized training in psychotherapy generally attends a training program at a psychotherapy institute.* The need for this training diminishes as the quality and relevance of the residency programs improve.

Membership in the American Psychiatric Association indicates professional responsibility but is not a sign of competence in psychotherapy. Physicians with one year of experience in psychiatry can join as associate members; those with three years can join as full members. Membership in psychotherapy or psychoanalytic associations is usually more meaningful.

If you are considering a psychiatrist, the more of the following credentials you find, the greater confidence you can have:

- Residency in psychiatry
- Full (not associate) membership in the American Psychiatric Association
- Board certification
- Graduation from a psychotherapy institute
- Membership in a psychotherapy or psychoanalytic society

Psychology The typical training of psychologists practicing psychotherapy consists of four years in graduate school with one year in an internship to get a PhD in clinical psychology. Clinical psychology programs include theoretical courses on personality and psychotherapy and supervised practicums in rendering psychotherapy. Some psychologists now obtain a PsyD (doctor of psychology) degree. This is a new practice-oriented degree offered in various mental health services, including psychotherapy. In most states, the title "psychologist" is controlled by law and only a person meeting certification or licensing requirements (usually a PhD in psy-

---

* Some psychotherapy institutes are known as psychoanalytic institutes, indicating a particular theoretical approach.

chology, two years supervised experience, passing special examinations) can call him/herself a psychologist. Some psychologists were certified or licensed under a "grandfather clause" if they had been in practice before the laws went into effect.

Not all psychologists are trained to do psychotherapy. Psychology has several other disciplines in addition to clinical psychology that incorporate clinical skills, such as school or counseling psychology, but many more disciplines which do not. While psychologists are legally free to work in all areas of the field, the American Psychological Association's code of ethics requires its members to function only in their area of competence.

Some clinical psychologists have diplomas awarded by the American Board of Examiners in Professional Psychology. This is the only board of all the professions that tests for competency in psychotherapy. Diplomas are awarded after the candidate has passed examinations that he/she is eligible to take after five years of postdoctoral experience. Relatively few clinical psychologists apply for the diplomate status although qualified to do so. Recognizing this reluctance and, wanting to meet the need for a directory of qualified psychotherapists, the Board of Examiners in 1975 developed a *National Register of Health Service Providers in Psychology*. All psychologists who are licensed or certified in their state, and have a PhD in psychology and two years of supervised experience (one postdoctoral) in mental health services, may be listed in the *Register*. These standards are relatively low, but the directory does provide that a psychologist has at least had some experience in offering mental health services, though not necessarily directly in psychotherapy.

Psychologists without clinical training can obtain such training by attending a training institute in psychotherapy. Clinical psychologists also attend such programs to further develop their psychotherapy skills.

Membership in the American Psychological Association, although of some protective value for clients because of its ethical restraints on members, is not a sign of psychotherapy competence. Membership in a psychotherapy or psychoanalytic association is more relevant to psychotherapy skills.

If you are considering a psychologist, check for the following credentials:

- A PhD in clinical psychology
- State certification or license
- Full membership in the American Psychological Association
- Graduation from a psychotherapy training institute
- Diplomate status in clinical psychology
- Membership in a psychotherapy or psychoanalytic association

Social Work The typical training for social workers is a master's degree (MSW) in social work, generally completed in a two-year program that includes field placement. It is possible to obtain a doctor's degree in social work (DSW) but very few social workers do. Social workers are certified (CSW) in their profession by many states on the basis of an MSW and passing an examination, and by the Academy of Certified Social Workers (ACSW) on the basis of the usual state requirements plus two years of supervised postdegree experience and an examination. Both certifications were awarded under a "grandfather clause" to already established social workers. The social work curriculum focuses on casework. Some schools offer a concentration in what used to be called psychiatric social work, with courses in personality, family interaction, and child development. This concentration also requires field placement in a mental health facility. The National Association of Social Workers publishes a *Register of Clinical Social Workers,* which lists ACSW members whose two years of post-master's experience was in clinical social work practice.

Social workers can go beyond the training offered in their field to get specialized training in psychotherapy. There are a number of training programs in psychotherapy, mostly in the large metropolitan areas, which accept people below the doctoral level.

Membership in the National Association of Social Workers is useful only as an indicator of professional responsibility with no bearing on psychotherapy skills, whereas membership in a psychotherapy or psychoanalytic association is relevant.

If you are considering a social worker check for the following credentials:

- Master's degree in social work with a clinical concentration
- Certification by state and/or Academy of Certified Social Workers
- Graduation from a psychotherapy or psychoanalytic training program
- Membership in a psychotherapy association

Nursing A fourth and emerging profession in psychotherapy is psychiatric nursing. To become a nurse one must graduate from a nursing program that includes training in psychiatry among other clinical areas. After graduation a nurse can become registered (RN) by passing state examinations. At present, there is no specialty licensing or certification for psychiatric nurses and any nurse can work as a psychiatric nurse.

A number of schools have begun to offer graduate training in psychiatric nursing, leading to a master's degree, and some to a PhD degree. This training includes courses on theoretical and practical aspects of psychotherapy.

In lieu of state certification, some state nursing associations grant a certificate in psychiatric nursing for members who have met specified training and experience requirements. The most stringent require a master's degree, including three semesters of supervised clinical work, personal therapy, and two years of supervised therapy experience after the master's degree.

Psychiatric nurses can also get specialized training in psychotherapy by attending a psychotherapy training institute. Membership in professional nursing associations is irrelevant to psychotherapy skills, but nurses trained in psychotherapy institutes can become members of psychotherapy associations.

If you are considering a psychiatric nurse, check for the following:

- A master's degree in psychiatric nursing
- Certification by the state nursing organization as a psychiatric nurse

- Graduation from a psychotherapy institute
- Membership in a psychotherapy association

Nonprofessional Therapists   An increasing number of therapists have been practicing without training or accreditation. Because the practice of psychotherapy is not controlled by law, anyone who wants to can offer psychotherapy services and use the title psychotherapist.

Therapists who practice without credentials usually come from one of two groups: those who believe their nonconformity represents a better way, and those who do it out of opportunism. The first are often principled persons with radical social philosophies. They shun the professions and training institutes because they consider such groups to be self-serving and socially regressive. They see clients' problems as stemming from the oppressiveness of society. Therapy to them is a process of education and political action. Although they do not deny the importance of skills, they believe that therapeutic skill consists of human qualities rather than technical expertise; a good therapist is simply a warm, open, and accepting person. Because they do not consider education in psychotherapy relevant, many have little or no training, although some have trained within "establishment" institutions and some have trained privately. Radical therapists work primarily at "alternate counseling centers," which aim to provide a new life pattern for counselors and clients. These centers, catering primarily to the needs of youth and minority groups, function as communities; members help each other and share experiences as well as fees. Many radical therapists also go into private practice.

For the other group, the opportunists, setting oneself up as a psychotherapist without having earned credentials is a shortcut to the status accorded the profession and to the possibility of a lucrative practice. This group reflects a range of different people and motives. Some may have started but not completed their training, some may have intentions of completing their training and becoming accredited, and some may be outright frauds with neither talent nor intentions to train.

Regardless of what group the therapist falls into, you

should be aware of the risks involved in being in therapy with a person who does not have recognized credentials. It is true that credentials by themselves are not enough to make a competent therapist, nor are they the ultimate criterion. But with the abundance of incompetent therapists, whether officially qualified or not, and the increasing occurrence of unethical practices, it is more important than ever that you have the added protection of working with a recognized practitioner. The accredited therapist practices under several regulatory bodies, including the state agency that sponsors his/her certificate or license, the ethics committee of the profession of which he/she is a member, and the judicial system through which legal action could be brought against him/her. Though in the past there has been infrequent action taken against a professional, the possibility thereof does function as a restraining influence. These sources of control do not exist for the nonaccredited therapist and it is not possible to prosecute a malpractice suit against someone who is not licensed to practice. Credentials do not ensure a good therapist, but do offer you some protection and recourse from abuse.

If you are considering a nonprofessional therapist, ask:

- What skills and capabilities does that person possess that can be helpful to you?
- What experience has he/she had doing therapy?
- Do the skills this person has to offer outweigh the added risks?

What Do All Those Titles Mean?

In addition to the titles of the major professions in psychotherapy, which have been discussed, people working in the field call themselves by many other titles as well. Below is a short rundown on various titles being used today, what they mean, and what kind of assurances, if any, they provide.

Psychotherapist Psychotherapist is a title anyone can use; it is not protected by law. It gives no indication of training or competence. Qualified practitioners sometimes use it as an adjunct to their professional title of psychiatrist, psychologist, et cetera. The term psychotherapist is also widely used by people without qualifications. If a person calls him/herself a psychotherapist without further clarification, be sure to probe on training, credentials, and approach to therapy.

Psychoanalyst This is another term that has no legal standing and can be used by anyone. Historically, a psychoanalyst was a person trained in classical Freudian theory and technique at a psychoanalytic institute. The term psychoanalysis today is used in two senses. Some use it to refer exclusively to Freudian analysis, while others use it to mean a specialized type of psychotherapy that goes more deeply into the roots of the personality structure and works more intensively, taking a longer period of time with a client. There are now many psychoanalytic institutes: some are Freudian, some are specific to other theories like Jungian or Sullivanian, while others are eclectic, not limiting themselves to any specific system. Some institutes (mostly Freudian), accept only physicians as students, while others accept students from other professions. As with the title psychotherapist, psychoanalyst gives no indication of competence, and is used by qualified and unqualified persons alike.

Marriage Counselor or Marriage Therapist These terms have no legal standing, except in California, and cover a multitude of practitioners and approaches. Although anyone can call him/herself a marriage counselor, the American Association of Marriage Counselors does set minimum standards for membership in its organization. Persons from a variety of professional backgrounds are admitted to membership, including psychology, social work, and medicine. Chances are, however, that a practitioner trained in one of these disciplines would identify him/herself by that profession rather than as a marriage counselor.

Family Counselor or Family Therapist These labels also have no legal standing. Some marriage and/or family therapists use the two terms interchangeably and see marriage therapy as part of family therapy. Family therapy usually refers to situations in which all members of the family are involved in the therapy process, often as a group. There are some training institutes for family therapy, and graduates from such centers should be suitably qualified.

Child Psychotherapist Another unprotected term, this

label tells you nothing and the practitioner may or may not have any relevant training and experience.

School Psychologist As already noted, psychologist is a title controlled by law, and a school psychologist has had to meet state licensing or certification requirements, including education, experience, and examinations. School psychologists generally work with children who have behavioral or academic difficulties at school and make referrals and recommendations for remediation or therapy.

Counselor, Guidance Counselor, Vocational Counselor Although graduate schools offer programs in counseling, these titles are not controlled by law and can be used by anyone. Career counselor is a more recent addition to titles in this area. These counselors generally provide specific advice in making vocational or career choices, but anyone, with or without training in this area, can use these titles.

Sex Therapist This title is open to use by anyone because it is not licensed or otherwise controlled. There has been a proliferation of organizations and individuals describing themselves as sex therapists, but only a small minority of these have any training or credentials in the field. "Sex therapy" has become a major area of abuse and unethical practices. Therefore, if you are considering seeing a sex therapist, it is important that you go to a practitioner who operates under some professional license, such as medicine or psychology, or to a clinic associated with an accredited hospital or university.

Therapist Personality and Personal Therapy

Training and credentials in psychotherapy are not enough to make a good therapist. A therapist must also have the personal characteristics that enable him/her to work closely with you in an atmosphere of mutual respect. The therapist has to have not only the ability to understand you and your problems, but also the sensitivity to communicate this understanding in a manner that is acceptable and meaningful to you. This makes you the only judge of the suitability of the therapist's personality to your needs. If you are not comfortable with the therapist, the therapy process cannot take place.

In our status-conscious society, we tend to be overly

impressed by experts and authorities. If you go into therapy with a shaky sense of your own self-worth, you are apt to accept as natural that the therapist sets the rules for your relationship and that you are expected to follow his/her cues. But this is not a genuine relationship and certainly not a therapeutic one. What you need is a therapist with whom you can feel at ease, someone with whom you do not have to screen your thoughts and feelings, someone whom you are not afraid to approach or to question. You should be able to enjoy and respect the therapist as a person—and know that the feeling is mutual.

What are some of the qualities you should look for? You need a therapist who is eager to know you as you are, not as a theory would have you. He/she should be genuinely concerned about your welfare, but in a supportive and non-restrictive manner. Respecting people's need to live in their own way, the therapist has to grant you, in therapy as well as out, the freedom to be what you want to be. The therapist should not be afraid of your feelings and anxieties. He/she has to be ready to stand by you and help you face them rather than shield you both from experiencing them. The therapist should be nonjudgmental of you as a person, but also ready to challenge you when you are not being true to yourself. A therapist has to be able to confront you in a positive manner, without hostility, derision, or sarcasm.

The therapist should also be expressive of his/her feelings and relate to you in a genuine way rather than hiding behind a mask of objective detachment. The therapist should not demand trust by virtue of his/her role, but earn it through his/her ability to be helpful and to respond to your needs. You want a therapist who can react in a spontaneous, natural way and is not too stiff to laugh. He/she should be able to recognize his/her own mistakes rather than deny them and pretend perfection.

Some psychotherapy systems hold that it is necessary for the therapist to stay removed and keep feelings hidden from view. This is not a constructive approach. Clients who have found their therapy helpful report that the therapist was a warm and caring person, while clients who did not find their therapy helpful report that the therapist was detached and aloof. Research studies on therapist personality characteristics that relate to positive results find that empathy (the ability to understand another person's feelings), warmth (care and concern for another), and genuineness (openness and directness) are the most important qualities. In one study conducted among clients in an outpatient clinic, "good" therapists were described as attentive, natural, and willing to engage in small talk, to give direct reassurance, to not be critical, and to not leave doubt about their real feelings; "bad" therapists were seen as making the individual feel like just another patient, as causing the patient to experience anger, as being passive and neutral, and using abstract language.

The therapy relationship is particularly prone to exploitation of clients, so you must be on guard to protect yourself from any destructive personal needs of the therapist. These often do not become very apparent until the therapy is under way, but there are several signs to watch out for. A therapist who "comes on strong," uses jargon, quick interpretations, or otherwise awes you with his/her brilliance, may need to use the relationship to build up self-importance at your expense. The therapist who takes over the sessions may derive satisfaction from being in an authoritarian role and, in so doing, keep you from emerging. The therapist who is overly friendly may need to entice you into a relationship that will feed his/her needs for admiration or intimacy. A therapist who is overly formal and aloof may use that role as an excuse for his/her incapacity to relate, and thereby will deprive you of a meaningful relationship.

Unresolved personal needs and a lack of maturity are suggested by a therapist's attempts to impress you with a particular "style." In the desire to win a client over, therapists have a tendency to take up whatever traits are in vogue. Some adopt an overly casual appearance to show they are not culture-bound; others are inappropriately informal, assuming the role of "good Joe" to show they are antiauthoritarian. Some indiscriminately use the latest methods to show they are professionally avant-garde, while others maintain whatever therapeutic style they were taught in school under the guise of professional rigor. Any of these stylized postures is a sign of a defensive rather than genuine approach to life and therapy. To become a real person, you need a therapist who is real.

Experiencing therapy personally is an important aspect of the therapist's preparation. Textbook familiarity with the process and techniques is not enough. Going through therapy enhances the therapist's ability to empathize with the client's feelings about going through therapy and, more importantly, helps the therapist understand his/her own limitations, fears, and ways of restricting life. It is essential for the therapist to appreciate fully personal feelings and defenses against them if he/she is to know when and how they interfere with the therapy. Although some people can have a lot of insight into themselves without the benefit of therapy, a therapist should not take the chance that such self-understanding is sufficient. Personal therapy also helps prepare therapists to deal with the emotional strains of their work. Therapists often engage in emotionally demanding encounters, immersing themselves in the clients' problems and becoming the butt of client feelings and accusations. The therapist not only has to accept these feelings but be able to turn them to therapeutic advantage. If the therapeutic interaction is not productive, therapists are apt to blame themselves and feel ineffectual. When that happens, therapists need enough inner strength to confirm a sense of self-worth. The nature of therapy demands that therapists live in close touch with their feelings. This closeness helps some live in greater harmony with themselves but for others it is a source of stress. There is evidence that not all psychotherapists have sufficiently strong foundations to withstand these emotional strains: the suicide rate among psychiatrists is disproportionately large, the highest of all the professions.

Despite the importance of personal therapy, not all therapists agree that it is necessary for themselves. There appears to be a difference among the professions in their attitudes toward this issue. Psychologists are more apt to have received therapy than psychiatrists and social workers. Of those psychiatrists who have had therapy, most report having done so for professional, or for a combination of professional and personal, reasons. In contrast, psychologists and social workers mostly sought out psychotherapy for personal reasons rather than viewing it primarily as a part of their training. Some therapists, like a lot of other people, think that they should not have personal therapy since this would be tantamount to saying that the therapist was just as "sick" as the clients. The old joke that you have to be crazy to see a psychotherapist is very much a part of that thinking. But a therapist who has not been in therapy may well be the one who is unwilling to face him/herself. And a therapist who claims to have had therapy for training purposes only (a "didactic analysis") has a need to make you think he or she is "healthy," thereby revealing an unbecoming defensive posture as well as a basic lack of understanding of what psychotherapy is about. It is highly unlikely that anyone who is unable, unwilling, or uninterested enough to get to know him/herself is going to be able to help you get to know yourself. Such a therapist is not going to be willing to explore his/her feelings as they relate to you either. Under these conditions you will not be able to experience your therapy as a genuine encounter between two persons, because one of them will be in hiding.

It may be that you want a therapist who has certain personal characteristics that you consider to be important for your therapy. For example, a lot of women today want only women therapists, many blacks want black therapists, many married people want married therapists. Some people feel that only an older therapist who has lived long enough to experience life's problems can be helpful, and others want a therapist who knows what it is like to live with children. If you have strong feelings about any such personal characteristic, feel free to look for a therapist who has what you want. There are, however, practical limits to what you will be able to find since therapists form a rather homogeneous group. Most are white, middle-aged men reared in middle-class urban areas, and a high proportion come from Jewish backgrounds. They tend to be politically liberal and nonreligious. Keep in mind, however, that similarity of experience is not as important as the therapist's ability to empathize with the meaning of those experiences to you. It is more important that you share basic values than common experiences. If a woman avoids a male therapist because she's afraid a man will try to push her into a passive "feminine" role and chooses instead a female therapist who then directs her into an active professional role, the client is not necessarily better off. With either of these therapists the consequences would be the same in that both would try to propel the client where they thought she belonged rather than exploring what was most appropriate to her. Similarity of background does not guarantee respect for your right to determine your own life.

Clinics and Training Centers

People tend to make unwarranted generalizations about clinics and training centers. A typical one is that you are safer in an organizational setting than with an independent practitioner because there is some control over the therapist: while you may not get the best, at least you won't get the worst. Another generalization is that clinics have lower fees, which in turn leads to the feeling that clinic therapists will not be very good.

Contrary to common belief, institutional status does not guarantee good or even acceptable standards for rendering service to the public. The requirements for an operating certificate are confusing and, once issued, the supervisory influence of the regulating state agency is usually minimal. As a matter of fact, clinics do not even have to be licensed to operate, though most are. That leaves the standards under which a clinic or psychotherapy center operates up to the institution's directorship. As a result, there are enormous variations in the quality of service provided by such institutions.

Psychotherapy clinics are the typical training grounds for therapists of all professions. The directors know that inexperienced therapists are less capable than experienced ones and, for that reason, reputable clinics provide intensive supervision for their less experienced staff members. Others, to maximize profits, seek out therapists with substandard qualifications who are willing to work for low fees and provide them with little or no supervision. The quality of supervision offered is often a major consideration in a therapist's decision to affiliate with one, rather than another, psychotherapy institution.

Although fees can be considerably lower at a clinic, some clinics charge just as much if not more than private practitioners. Similarly, while circumstances favor getting a relatively inexperienced therapist in a clinic, this is not always the case either. Not all therapists at clinics are beginners in training. For different reasons, some therapists prefer to stay at a clinic rather than going into independent practice, even though their apprenticeship is over and they have acquired the necessary experience and accreditation. Some psychotherapy centers, especially those affiliated with advanced training institutions, maintain high standards, selecting therapists who already have substantial prior qualifications. Such therapists, though still in a training capacity, may possess qualifications superior to those of some independent practitioners.

Clinics also vary in the kind of psychotherapy service they render. Some, particularly those connected with advanced training institutions, want to provide their trainees with experience in intensive psychotherapy and prefer to accept clients who are ready to commit themselves to long-term therapy. Clinics connected with universities are usually eclectic in orientation and those affiliated with analytic training schools (such as Freudian, Jungian, and so on) specialize in their particular approach. Most unaffiliated psychotherapy clinics encompass a variety of psychotherapy approaches. Of late, some clinics have adopted behaviorist methods and a few even specialize in them.

Clinics affiliated with hospitals are generally of one of two types. Most are "outpatient" clinics that operate close to the medical model. Though psychotherapy may be offered to various degrees, these clinics are inclined toward psychiatric methods, including drug and shock treatment. They tend to draw seriously disturbed persons who anticipate a need for medical treatment. Some teaching hospitals, on the other hand, have psychoanalytic training institutes with associated clinics that are specifically geared to rendering psychotherapy.

Social service, religious, and charitable organizations sometimes offer psychotherapy, but generally their services are limited to the more practical problems of living. Crisis centers specialize in sudden, transitory upsetting experiences in life including, but not limited to, suicidal urges. With the recent interest in family therapy, centers have emerged specializing in that approach. They focus on working with the whole family, prefering to treat it as a unit rather than through its individual members.

The anxiety of having to make choices is in no way bypassed by going to a clinic. The danger of your falling into the wrong situation is just as great as with an independent practitioner. It might be easier to find a clinic than an independent practitioner since clinics are allowed to publicize their services, whereas independent practitioners (that is, those who stick to professional practices) are not. But when you find a psychotherapy clinic that seems to be right for you, you still have to assess its quality. While some clinics are good, many exist primarily as money-making operations. It is reasonable to generalize that chances for obtaining good psychotherapy are better at a clinic that has accreditation from an appropriate state agency and is affiliated with a well-known training institution like a university.

Even after finding a suitable psychotherapy institution, you still have to select the therapist or, if you are not given choices, at least approve of him/her. The usual procedure at such institutions is for you to have an "intake" interview conducted by a social worker, after which you are assigned to a particular therapist. Sometimes these assignments are made with special consideration for your needs and sometimes on purely administrative grounds. If you have any special preferences for a therapist, this is the time to make them known. The same basic requirements discussed earlier apply just as well to therapists in a clinic as to those in independent practice. If the therapist does not meet all of the training requirements, you can find out if he/she is in the process of completing training and working under the active supervision of a fully qualified practitioner in the meantime. If the therapist is not a person you like or feel comfortable with, you will have to ask to be assigned to someone more acceptable to you.

Most psychotherapy institutions keep records on you. If licensed, they are generally required to do so. A file is kept on each client, usually including diagnosis, summaries of the intake interview and of subsequent sessions, progress reports, and termination reports. Clinics vary in the extent to which the privacy of these records is guarded. In some, they are used with proper discretion and serve only supervisory purposes on the part of either the clinic's management or the state accreditation agency. In others, the records are used with less discretion for research, training, or demonstration purposes. You have a right to ask what information is being recorded and to know who has access to your file.

Fees and Insurance

Money is one of the factors that is bound to influence your choice of a therapist. Fees charged for psychotherapy vary widely, but most psychotherapists in private practice charge between $25 and $50 per session. Substantially higher fees are charged by well-established or prominent psychotherapists. Psychotherapists whose clientele comes from a moneyed field, such as the entertainment world, also maintain higher fees in accord with the income of the people with whom they deal. In smaller communities, less prominent therapists are apt to charge higher fees because there is less competition. Fees under $25 are obtainable mostly in clinics. Some clinics with a sliding fee scale offer psychotherapy for as little as $1 or $2 per session, although others charge more than $25. Many therapists in private practice also adjust their fee to the client's financial status, but usually within a fairly limited range, such as 10 percent or 20 percent of the regular fee.

Fees vary by professional background, though these differences are narrowing. Psychiatrists as a group charge more than psychologists as a group, and the latter charge more than social workers. This fee differential stems, in part, from the salary hierarchies among the professions in institutional settings. Since most mental health institutions are based on the medical model, they pay the highest salaries to physicians. Another reason is the public's willingness to pay higher fees to psychiatrists because of the medical mystique. A recent study of psychotherapy in the metropolitan Washington, D.C., area showed average fees charged for individual sessions to be $39 for psychiatrists, $34 for psychologists, and $26 for social workers. The average fees for group therapy sessions were $19, $18, and $16 respectively.

The size of the fee is not necessarily a measure of competence. The low fee structure of a clinic can include an unusually talented though not yet established therapist as well as an inexperienced student. The middle range of fees can include a beginner in independent practice trying to bluff his/her way into the image of an established practitioner or a very accomplished but modest practitioner. The high fee therapist can have special talents or may possibly just be a good entrepreneur.

If you choose a therapist with a low fee, the chances are that his/her experience or training will be limited. If this is the case, be sure that such lacks are compensated for through active supervision and continued training. Your attitude toward low-priced services is also important. If you feel that a "cheap" therapist can't be good, that attitude, although unrealistic, may impede the therapy more than any limitations in the therapist's training or experience.

If you can afford it, it is probably best to choose a therapist in the middle range since he/she is apt to have solid qualifications at a reasonable cost. It will still be necessary for you to check this out. If a high-priced therapist does not have specialized capabilities important to you, be careful not to choose such a therapist for snob appeal—that's just as poor a basis for choosing a therapist as it is for going to therapy. Do not pay for reputation or image, but for quality of services. Also, remember that fees are often negotiable. If you like a therapist but the fee is too high, do not be afraid to ask if the therapist will see you for less.

Many major medical and health insurance policies cover part of psychotherapy expenses. If you want to start therapy, check out your policies to see if you have coverage. If you do not have insurance that includes psychotherapy benefits, it is possible that you might qualify through the policy of a spouse or parent. The kind of coverage provided by these policies varies greatly. Some provide very limited benefits and others pay up to several thousands of dollars. Some policies insure only for psychotherapy rendered in a hospital setting, but many cover office visits. Some cover psychotherapy only if administered by a psychiatrist or another physician, some cover for psychologists and physicians, and others cover for psychologists only if referral has been made by a physician. About half of the states have passed "freedom of choice" legislation that requires insurance companies to reimburse policyholders for psychotherapy rendered by psychologists. At this time, neither social workers nor psychiatric nurses are included, except for some policies expressly written for organizations composed of members of those professions. Because of legal precedents, some insurance companies currently allowed by state laws to restrict psychotherapy benefits to policyholders who see medical practitioners have reimbursed for psychologists' services when requested.

Medicare pays only for psychotherapy services rendered by physicians. Medicaid benefits vary from county to county. In some areas they cover only treatment administered by physicians but in others they cover psychotherapy with psychologists.

The cost of psychotherapy is deductible as a medical expense on income tax returns when rendered by either medical or nonmedical practitioners.

The inclusion of insurance and tax benefits under medical services perpetuates the medical model of psychotherapy. Since, understandably, neither clients or practitioners want to lose out on these benefits, both parties engage in a bit of hypocrisy when claiming them as "medical services." This will continue for as long as psychotherapy benefits are available only under the medical umbrella.

How to Find Names

Several different procedures can be followed to find names of potential therapists in your area. One good way of getting names is from friends and acquaintances who have been in therapy, since they can also give you an advance description of the therapist. Still, therapists are not always the same with each client and there is no guarantee that a friend's favorable experience will be repeated.

Physicians, although frequently used in this capacity, are not apt to be a good referral source. They often belittle psychotherapy, want to treat your problems medically, or try doing psychotherapy themselves. If they do refer, it is likely to be to a psychiatrist even though a therapist from another profession might be more suitable for you. Of course, some physicians do make appropriate referrals, but you should be alert to the possible pitfalls of this source. Psychotherapists, being more knowledgeable about psychotherapy, are a better source for referrals, but they too are inclined to favor practitioners who share a similar therapeutic orientation or come from the same professional background.

A good way of getting a referral is to consult a leading figure in the field who knows lots of therapists, such as the director of a psychotherapy training institute. That person should be able to make a well-considered referral based on knowledge of both the field and many therapists, graduates as well as students. If such a person is not available to you, or you don't want to pay for a personal consultation, you can still call one or more training institutes and they will probably be happy to give you the names of graduates or refer you to somebody still in training at the institute.

You can call the local professional society for psychiatrists, psychologists, social workers, or psychiatric nurses. They usually give you names of three practitioners in your area and sometimes respond to more specific requests for information about the therapist's services, fees, or years of practice. Names can also be found by consulting directories of the various professional organizations. First decide which professional background comes closest to your philosophical predispositions so you can check in the appropriate directory. Psychiatrists are listed in the *American Psychiatric Association Directory,* or in the *Directory of Medical Specialists* if they are certified; psychologists will be found in the *American Psychological Association Directory* and the *National Register of Health Service Providers in Psychology*; and social workers are listed in the membership directory of the National Association of Social Workers or in its *Register of Clinical Social Workers.* The directories, usually available in large public libraries, have a geographical listing where you can first check who lives in the area you want, and then read the biographical entry.

The *Yellow Pages* are primarily useful in providing the names of practitioners in your area, but these names will require further checking. Psychiatrists are not listed separately from "Physicians and Surgeons" and the psychologist and social worker columns do not give the specialty. None of the names are screened for licenses or qualifications, and the lists are not comprehensive because many qualified practitioners do not list themselves in classified telephone books. Psychotherapy clinics are listed under "Clinics" alongside abortion and medical centers and again require further checking on your part.

Of late, there has been a burgeoning of "referral services" in some large cities. These services place ads in the classified sections of various magazines and newspapers under headings such as "Personal" or "Counseling," or in the *Yellow Pages* under "Clinics." Some referral services were organized by psychotherapy associations as a means of providing the public with a source of qualified practitioners; others are a front for one or more psychotherapists who are seeking additional clientele. It is a violation of the ethical standards of the professions to advertise or otherwise solicit clients, but one can get around this restriction by advertising a referral service, which then refers clients to the parties who have established this front. Psychotherapists affiliated with such referral services may or may not be qualified to practice.

In addition to the advertisements for referral services, ads have been appearing in which individual "psychotherapists" or "psychoanalysts" advertise directly. These are almost certainly placed by nonaccredited therapists because accredited therapists, in so doing, risk the loss of their credentials by violating professional ethics.

Though advertising one's services is currently a violation of professional ethics, this may not be true in the future. A trend is under way, already initiated for lawyers, to permit professionals to advertise as a public service. These ads would be limited to essential information required by the public, such as the nature of service rendered and fees charged for it.

4.
The First Interview

THE PURPOSE OF THE FIRST SESSION IS FOR YOU AND the therapist to explore the desirability of working together, not to start therapy. When you sense a need for therapy, try to make arrangements for the first session as early as possible. If you wait, the pressure of your needs may become too great to use the screening process to good advantage. Taking the time and effort to make sure you will be in the right therapy setting will pay handsome dividends later on; without that assurance you will not have a valid basis for committing yourself fully to the therapy process.

The "first session" may not be limited to one visit. The term is used to mean all the initial sessions required for you to decide whether a particular therapist is right for you. That may take one, two, or three sessions, sometimes more.

The Initial Phone Contact
Typically, people leave for the first session what should be clarified before scheduling it. When you call for an appointment it is perfectly all right to ask for more than a time and a date. There are several things you want to know before even making an appointment. Unless you are making an appointment for just a single consulting session, the first thing to know is if the therapist has time to see you on a regular basis. Sometimes a therapist will make an appointment to see you and then inform you once you are in the office that his/her schedule is booked up for further appointments. In such an eventuality, you might have to wait for

weeks or months before being able to schedule regular appointments. You also want to ask if the therapist has hours available that are manageable for you. Otherwise, you might not find out until you are in the office that you can start therapy only if you can come at 7:00 A.M. one day and 10:00 P.M. the next. Another important piece of information is the therapist's fee. There is no reason why you should not ask this beforehand and no valid reason why the therapist should not answer. If you cannot afford to continue at a particular fee, there is no sense setting up an appointment in the first place (unless you intend only a single consultation for an opinion or a referral). Some therapists may not want to discuss the fee over the phone because their fee is negotiable, preferring first to find out your financial circumstances. In this case, they can indicate their range of fee.

You can also ask the therapist about his/her qualifications and therapy approach: what kind of training has he/she had, is he/she a Jungian, a Gestaltist, a behavior modifier, engaged in individual therapy only or in group therapy as well, and so forth. Feel free to ask any question that is pertinent to the type of service the therapist can provide.

Many therapists will avoid answering your questions on the phone. While there are some questions that do not belong in a phone conversation, those that are relevant to the type of service you can expect to receive should be taken up before you make an office visit. Factual answers to information-seeking questions indicate that the therapist wants to help you make an informed decision on whether or not to contemplate starting therapy with him/her. Refusal to answer may indicate that the therapist feels you do not have a right to the information, or that you are only entitled to the information if you first pay for his/her time. Therapists have a right to refuse to answer questions that do not relate to the services they provide. They also cannot answer questions that require a prior familiarity with you as, for example, whether therapy will be helpful for you or how long it can be expected to take. And, of course, you should keep the amount of time you expect the therapist to spend on the phone with an unknown person to a reasonable limit.

When you want to see a psychotherapist, it is important that you make the initial telephone inquiry yourself. You might feel tempted to delegate the task to a spouse or friend if you feel very anxious about it. If someone else calls for you, and the psychotherapist agrees to make an appointment in this fashion, you and the therapist are starting off on the wrong foot by letting others do for you what you might be able to do on your own. You may want somebody else to arrange the initial appointment because it is that person's idea that you go into therapy. If this is the case, and the therapist allows another person to deputize for you, you and the therapist are agreeing that you should enter therapy against your wish. If at all possible, get on the phone yourself.

When you make an initial telephone inquiry, it is also important that the therapist speak to you directly. It is best to get the answers to important issues, such as future availability or fees, from the therapist rather than from a secretary or receptionist. In a clinic or other institutional setting, you will not be able to arrange an appointment directly with the therapist, but try to obtain the necessary information from the person who handles your call.

First Impressions

Having gotten over the hurdle of setting up a first appointment, the next task is to conduct the first interview. It is a mistake to think that once you are in the therapist's office you have nothing further to do except sit back and let the therapist take over. You both have to get acquainted with each other and find out what each expects of the other. It is your task to let the therapist know what your problems are and what you expect from therapy. It is also your job to evaluate the therapist and get a sense of your feelings about working with that person. Finally, it is your task to explore the terms on which the therapist is offering his/her services and to weigh their acceptability to you. The therapist should be using this period to explore the nature of your problem and his/her feelings about working with you.

The first interview differs depending on whether you go to a clinic or to a private practitioner. In a clinic, it is conducted by an administrator—sometimes the clinic director, but usually a social worker trained in "intake" procedures. The "intake interview" usually follows a predetermined pattern in which you will be asked to provide information regarding your present situation, original family composition, medical history, sexual history, developmental milestones and, last but not least, your "presenting problem," which means the problem that is bringing you to therapy. The interview is not set up primarily as a means for you and the clinic mutually to explore needs and expectations; rather, it is structured to obtain data from you that will be used to make a diagnosis, assess your suitability to the clinic, and acquaint the therapist with you beforehand. It is not necessary for you to go along sheepishly with the interviewing procedure and answer all questions put to you. If you have reason not to discuss certain issues in an intake interview, feel free to say so. Some clinics will question you on your preferences in therapist assignment but most will assign you to a therapist on a basis of administrative factors rather than therapist-client matching. Whether a clinic does or does not spontaneously give you an opportunity to express your wants, do not hesitate to do so. It may or may not be possible to grant your preferences, but if you do not specify what you want, no attempt can be made.

When you see a private practitioner, your first impression will be gleaned from the waiting room and office. Take it in, but don't get carried away by appearances. Of course a person is reflected in his/her choice of surroundings, but some therapists rent furnished office space in professional buildings, share offices and decorate by mutual consent, or sublet offices from other therapists. In these instances office furnishings tend to be nondescript, which does not necessarily mean that the therapist is similarly bland. Some therapists deliberately keep the surroundings neutral and simple. Individuality in decor may indicate that the therapist does not feel it is intrusive if his/her personal tastes are apparent, or that the therapist wants you to notice his/her taste. When an office is decorated in an extreme manner, it becomes obvious that the therapist wants to make a statement about him/herself. You will have to decide if you feel the furnishings are there to keep you and the therapist comfortable, or to impress you.

Some people put much weight on the reading matter in the waiting room and the number of books on the wall in the office. Again, if therapists share a waiting room you do not know who is subscribing to what. You also do not know what is left by other clients. The books on the wall may indicate that the therapist is well read, or that he/she wants you to have that impression. Lack of books does not mean the therapist does not read. He/she may prefer to keep the books at home, or to borrow them from the public library. To assess the therapist more accurately you have to do a lot of questioning and be observant of the manner in which the answers, or lack of answers, are conveyed.

Some therapists practice in their homes. If there is a separate office with a private entrance it makes little difference that the space happens to be in a home. In other cases, an office in the therapist's house or apartment may be reached through a common entrance with the family or may even be living quarters of the home, most often the living room. Clients are usually not neutral about such arrangements, and either like the idea a lot or take to it badly. Either reaction bodes difficulties. Those who like the idea usually feel that it brings them close to the therapist, but deriving comfort from an assumed personal relationship with the therapist risks diverting you from the purpose of coming to therapy. If you do not like the idea of seeing a therapist in a home setting, then it is obvious that this is not a suitable arrangement for you. If you do not have a strong reaction either way, then there is no reason why such an arrangement cannot work out, provided that the personal life of the therapist does not intrude on your time before, during, or after sessions.

Having gleaned some impressions from the physical arrangements, the next step is to enter the office and take a seat. If there is more than one place to sit, the therapist may let you gravitate to the one that suits you best, or invite you to take a particular chair or spot on the couch. A big difference between the comfort of seating for the therapist and client may indicate feelings of the therapist toward the client. On the other hand, a very comfortable chair is important for the therapist who probably sits in it most of the day. If the therapist sits behind a desk, he/she is creating a distance between you and subtly defining a stance and your relative places in the relationship. The desk helps to foster the impression that you are the object to be studied by the authority; it does not suggest that you are both there mutually to explore each other.

Defining Problems and Goals

It is best to make it clear from the start that your purpose in the first session is to explore the possibilities of working together. Despite what the therapist may assume, you are not there to start therapy but to see if there is a basis for starting. After this clarification, the therapist may wait for you to begin or may start the session him/herself. In that case, a suitable question is "What makes you interested in therapy?" or "What brings you here?" If the therapist does not open the interview you can, by describing your problems and what you want to get from therapy. The therapist will probably ask questions to elucidate the nature of the problem, the way it is experienced, and its origins. Some therapists may ask questions you feel are not relevant to your problem or even avoid the problem as you have presented it, preferring to conduct a standard intake interview instead. In this event do not feel coerced into providing all the information requested—give only what you consider appropriate. If the therapist insists on knowing, inquire how giving that information at this particular time will be helpful to you. Provide the information if the answer makes sense but do not accept as an answer simply that the therapist must have all the information requested.

Some therapists go through a long list of routine questions so that they can make a psychiatric diagnosis (anxiety neurosis, obsessive-compulsive, manic-depressive, et cetera), which then determines what kind of treatment you will get. By giving you a label the therapist relates to you as a representative of a certain diagnostic category rather than as a human being with unique problems. R. D. Laing has called psychiatric diagnosis, with its dehumanization of the client, a "degradation ceremonial."

After clarifying the nature of your problem(s) and the expectations you have of therapy, ask the therapist for his/her reactions. What happens in the actual therapy process will, of course, be influenced by what is revealed about you in the course of the therapy itself. However, each therapist is going to have immediate reactions to you and the problems you present, and plans on how to proceed. Ask the therapist to be as specific as possible on these points: Does the therapist accept the dimensions of the problem as you outline it or does he/she perceive other difficulties you have not presented? How does the therapist envisage the course of therapy —what is the therapist's feeling about the amount of time that will be needed to approach your goals, and about the most desirable frequency of sessions? Does the therapist want to work with you on a one-to-one basis or have you join a therapy group now or in the future? If this has not been determined before, to what particular school of therapy does the therapist subscribe (psychoanalytic, Gestalt, behavior modification), and what approach and methods can you expect in the course of therapy?

If the therapist should recommend drug or electric shock therapy either as adjuncts to or as a substitute for psychotherapy, be on guard. These procedures entail a much greater risk to both your mental and your physical well-being than psychotherapy. If any mood-affecting drugs, including tranquilizers, are recommended on other than a temporary basis, it is wise to get a second professional opinion. If you consent to such treatment, be sure that you get, or have recently had, a medical checkup to lessen the chances of undesirable side effects. Psychoactive drugs or shock treatment should not be prescribed without first obtaining a complete medical history, including a list of other medications being taken and of allergies. Similarly, obtain instructions on what other medications or food to avoid while taking the drugs and what possible side effects to watch out for.

Some therapists, no matter how you try to define your purpose in the first session, are going to take it for granted that you are there to start therapy. That may be what is happening if the therapist prematurely attempts to gain a detailed case history, interrupts your presentation of the problems you want to work on by focusing on one particular issue, and does not give you the opportunity to ask questions about the therapy. If a therapist assumes that therapy has begun, make sure that you let the therapist know if you are still in the process of evaluating that possibility.

During the course of stating your problems, you may find the therapist offering you interpretations of your behavior that are unwarranted on the basis of the information you have presented. This sometimes happens when the therapist wants to impress the client with his/her ability to size up the situation quickly. It is usually the sign of an insecure therapist who needs to show off. It may also be the therapist's way of getting the therapy process started before you have decided that he/she is the person with whom you want to start. While the therapist should provide you with his/her impressions as to the nature of your problem, such interpretations do not belong in a first interview.

The therapy relationship is grounded on some very concrete conditions, which the therapist may or may not clarify spontaneously. These concern not only the goals toward which you will work and the methods to be used, but also the arrangements under which therapy will be carried out, including appointments, fees, and confidentiality, all of which are discussed in the next chapter. If these issues are not brought up by the therapist, you must raise them on your own. They have to be understood beforehand and be acceptable to you. If you feel that the terms of the therapy relationship are oppressive or unfair, this is bound to interfere with the work that you can do together.

Exploring Therapist Qualifications

If you don't have enough information about the therapist's qualifications before coming to the first session, you can fill in the gaps at that time. Unfortunately, many therapists are defensive on this issue and hide behind various rationalizations to avoid having to give clients direct answers about themselves. One well-known textbook for practitioners suggests that when a client requests specific information, such as how many years the therapist has been practicing, all the client wants is reassurance of the therapist's competence and, therefore, only has to be told that the therapist feels competent to work with him/her. Such avoidance of a direct answer expresses an attitude of contempt for the client. The same textbook suggests that, since clients have no basis for evaluating therapist competency, if a client persists in requesting specific information the therapist should comment on the "unusual nature of their behavior," which must have "some underlying meaning": "Perhaps a generalized need to have more information than should be necessary for making decisions is one of their neurotic difficulties, or perhaps they characteristically antagonize people by refusing to take what is said to them at face value, or perhaps they are having second thoughts about continuing in psychotherapy or about their ability to be helped." * Here, the request for pertinent information is turned against the client, who is made to feel there is something wrong with him/her for wanting to know rather than with the therapist for refusing to tell.

A therapist who does not want to answer questions about qualifications shows an inappropriate defensiveness and a lack of respect for you that does not augur well for a productive therapeutic relationship. Further, if the therapist implies that there is something wrong with you for asking such questions, you have come to the wrong office and had better start looking again.

Therapist Characteristics and Values

If you have strong feelings about any particular characteristic of the therapist such as sex, age, religion, or his/her personal values, and you sense that they might interfere with your therapy, discuss them with the therapist. You should not start therapy until you are satisfied that you are informed about that particular issue or your concern is put at rest. Here again, as with qualifications, you may run into difficulties getting the information you want. Some therapists feel it is harmful to the therapy to provide any personal information about themselves. (The reasons for this are discussed in chapter 8, "Feelings About the Therapist.") If the therapist refuses to answer your questions you will have to judge whether it is a rigid refusal on principle, an arrogant refusal of your right to question the therapist, a defensive self-

* Irving B. Weiner, *Principles of Psychotherapy* (New York: John Wiley, 1975), p. 83.

protective refusal, or a well-thought-out refusal based on genuine hesitations about your particular situation.

You and the therapist should share basic values and goals in life. When questioned about their values, many therapists will dismiss the question, answering that their values do not enter into their work. If so, they are not very perceptive about what they are doing in the therapy process. The basic values of the therapist cannot help but influence the therapist's approach to you. Clients are often concerned about issues such as homosexuality, politics, women's rights, or drug use. If any such issues are important to you, it is legitimate to ask where the therapist stands. If a therapist responds that he/she thinks you should do whatever you want just so long as it does not hurt others, the therapist is avoiding discussing his/her values. Ultimately you and the therapist will have to come to grips with the value questions you are raising; it is better sooner than later.

Sensing the Vibrations

In the course of discussing your problems and asking the therapist questions you will be able to start forming impressions about the therapist. Are you getting positive "vibes"? Is the therapist a person you respect and someone with whom you feel comfortable? Do you like the therapist, and does the feeling seem to be mutual?

Do you think the therapist can help you? Does the therapist accept your right to ask questions or discourage your inquiries? Do your questions lead to satisfying interactions and a furthering of understanding? Does the therapist make you feel that what you have to say is important, or does he/she take a patronizing air with you? Does the therapist talk to you in a way that is meaningful to you?

Does the therapist seem to have the characteristics necessary for successful psychotherapy? Is the therapist sensitive and able to understand you, does he/she seem to be concerned about you, and does he/she strike you as a genuine person free of defensive affectations?

Do you trust what the therapist says, or is the therapist trying to impress you with professional jargon, forced friendliness, or exaggerated promises of a "cure"?

Is the therapist free of signs such as nervous tics, strained voice, or awkward mannerisms suggesting excessive tensions, inadequate self-control, or other personal problems? Smoking (discussed in chapter 6, "Sore Spots") also falls into this category.

To answer these questions, take stock of your observations and immediate reactions to the therapist. Do not be afraid to trust your impressions; your feelings are the best guide available to you. If, from your experience with the therapist, you sensed that he/she is genuine, responsive, warm, and able to understand you, most likely that person is genuine, responsive, warm, and able to understand you. If you sensed that the therapist is abrupt, cold, and disrespectful, he/she probably is abrupt, cold, and disrespectful. Do not dismiss any feelings you had about the therapist. If some are not clear, explore them in subsequent sessions.

End-of-Session Options

When you have finished the first session you may or may not want to schedule another. Remember that it is up to you to ask or not to ask for another appointment. Do not let the therapist take this choice away from you. Several options are open to you:

- If your impressions about the therapist are so clearly negative that you are sure you do not want to continue with that person, do not hesitate to tell the therapist that you do not want to come back. Feel free to say why if you want to.
- If your feelings about the therapist are mixed and you are not sure whether or not you want to return, tell the therapist about your uncertainty and that you will phone again if you want to continue. You may find that given some time to reflect about the therapist you will be able to reach a decision. Or, you might want to interview another therapist and see if you come away feeling better about your prospects.
- If your feelings about the therapist are positive but you need more time to discuss all that is important in making a decision, tell the therapist that you would like more time to explore the possibilities with him/her and set up another appointment.

- If your feelings about the therapist are clearly positive, and you definitely want to start therapy, set up a schedule of appointments and consider yourself on the way.

Sometimes therapists or clients arrange for a "trial period" of therapy. A trial period means that although both parties agree to work together, the relationship is considered to be tentative until experience shows that both parties can work productively together.

Should the therapist tell you that you have to make an on-the-spot decision about continuing if you want to have hours open for you, do not feel pressured into going along when you still have doubts. Such pressure in itself constitutes a lack of sensitivity to your legitimate concerns.

Checklist for First Session

- Did the therapist facilitate relating your problems and reasons for coming to therapy? Does he/she seem to understand what you were talking about? Do you feel comfortable with the therapist?
- Are you and the therapist in general agreement on problem areas and expectations for the therapy? Is his/her concept of therapy compatible with yours?
- If the therapist wants to include drugs, do you agree and are you taking proper safeguards?
- Does the therapist have a "therapeutic" personality: competent, sincere, and responsive? Is he/she free of obvious signs indicating excessive nervousness or emotional disturbance?
- Did you check out the therapist's qualifications, training, experience, personal therapy, credentials?
- Did the therapist answer your questions, whether about you or the therapist, adequately?
- Did you work out contractual issues, including time and fees, to your satisfaction?

5.
The Therapy Agreement

THERAPY IS A RELATIONSHIP BETWEEN TWO PEOPLE IN which each has certain legitimate expectations of the other and obligations to the other. Clients usually know that they are supposed to show up for sessions, present material for therapy, and pay for each session. But clients are vague about what else therapists expect from them and what they can and should expect from therapists. They are not clear about how they and the therapist will work together, what methods the therapist will use, and, more importantly, if their work together is oriented toward the client's goals. Therapists, on the other hand, do have goals and operating procedures in mind, but they usually do not clarify them for the client. A therapy agreement based on mutual consent offers protection to both you and the therapist. By clarifying the conditions of therapy, an agreement reduces the chances of the therapy relationship going on the rocks and it can even offer some legal protection should that ever become necessary. You and the therapist can work meaningfully together only if you are agreed beforehand on the goals, methods, and arrangements of the therapy.

An agreement also establishes the principle of mutual accountability as the basis of the therapeutic relationship. It places you in a responsible role in the therapy relationship from the outset by recognizing that you and the therapist must define the goals and conditions of therapy together. If at a later date either of you finds the terms of your agreement cumbersome, it will be easier to change them because the process of reaching mutually acceptable conditions has already been established.

Discussing the terms of your therapy relationship before you start therapy makes it more likely that you will come to a suitable agreement. After you start, your emotional investment in the therapy will reduce your freedom to negotiate. Not only do you want an agreement, but the process of discussing it is an excellent way of learning at an early point how well you and the therapist can work together.

There are three major areas in which you want to spell out your rights and obligations: the goals toward which you will work, the methods that will be used, and the arrangements under which the therapy will be carried out.

Agreeing on Goals

Unless you have stated what your goals and objectives are in coming to therapy, and unless the therapist agrees to work with you toward these goals, you may find the therapy running into difficulties later on. It often happens that a client comes to therapy with limited goals and that the therapist pushes the client to work toward more rewarding objectives. In such a case, although the therapist is working toward what he/she conceives as the client's best interests, this private agenda may not coincide with the client's self-perceived problems. A therapist should certainly let a client know if he/she thinks a particular set of goals is restrictive, but he/she has the obligation to work toward the goals the client has set. If the therapist feels that these goals are not legitimate or inclusive enough, the therapist has the responsibility to explain this, and if the client still does not agree, the therapist should not work with that particular person.

While the basis of working together is agreement on what is being worked toward, this does not mean that either the client or therapist cannot suggest a change in goals at any given point. Both parties are free to bring up the question of goals when they think it is called for. If the goals are then modified, it represents a change in the agreement because it is done with the explicit understanding of both parties.

Agreeing on Methods

Before reaching the therapist's office, you will probably have formed some opinions on the types of approaches and techniques you feel are most meaningful to you. You should also know beforehand what methods the therapist will want to use. Do not consider yourself obligated to engage in any type of behavior that you do not find acceptable or to accept any later innovations that you have not agreed on. It is desirable to have a clear statement in the agreement on all issues that are important to you. The most common areas of concern about methods are:

- Will your therapy be essentially a verbal process, or does the therapist want to introduce any acting or body techniques? Does he/she insist on your following through with such techniques?
- Does the therapist want you to use a chair, or the couch, or is that choice open to you?
- Does the therapist expect you to join a group now or at some later time? Does the therapist have a group you can join if you should want to, or will he/she help you find a group?
- Does the therapist expect you to see anyone else, such as a physician for a medical checkup or a psychologist for diagnostic evaluation?
- Will the therapist want you to use medication if you become very anxious or depressed, or will the therapist want you to avoid such medication? If you do not agree with the therapist on the role of medication in psychotherapy, will the therapist respect your choice or insist that you follow his/her position?
- Does the therapist want to interview other members of your family? Will the therapist do so if you should make such a request? Is the therapist willing to work with other members of your family if you want to augment your personal therapy with marital or family therapy?

It is not possible to specify in advance the host of techniques that may be desirable during the course of your therapy. Nor is it necessary. However, you should have a fairly clear idea as to how you will be expected to work with your therapist and you should find these procedures agreeable.

As with goals, it may become desirable to change the ways of working in your therapy at some point. For instance, a particular method previously not considered may become appropriate later on because you have become more open or because the therapist has acquired a new skill. Sometimes a change in goals calls for a change in method: if the focus of therapy moves from the broad goal of insight development to the specific goal of becoming more assertive, a change from nondirective techniques such as free association to more active encounter techniques would be in order. An agreement does not preclude such changes. It can always be amended and, in fact, helps to clarify the changes that you want.

Agreeing on Arrangements

Duration   While it is impossible to specify exactly how long your therapy will take, an agreement can specify the length of time you and the therapist want to work together before reviewing, and possibly renegotiating, the terms of your agreement.

The length of time agreed upon may depend on your goals, how long the therapy is expected to take, and your degree of confidence in the therapist. As a general rule, an agreement should be for a period of not less than three months and not more than a year. A period shorter than three months is usually not a sufficient amount of time in which to get much accomplished, and a period of more than a year does not automatically provide for periodic review of the therapy relationship. Though many therapies will last for more than one year, the one-year agreement can be renewed as often as desirable. You will have to discuss with the therapist if he/she is willing to work on a specified short-term basis, if that is what you want, or on an indefinite time basis with annual renewal of your agreement.

The duration of therapy should be discussed with the therapist even though it cannot be specified in the agreement. The only meaningful way to estimate duration is in terms of what you hope to accomplish within the therapy process. The time required depends also on your accessibility to the therapy process and how hard you work at it. The more open you are to your feelings and the more determined you are, the faster your therapy will move along. Similarly, the therapist's capabilities and compatability with you will influence the duration of therapy. Some people feel that the "action therapies" cut down the length of time required for the therapy process, but there is no evidence that they do. There is, however, some indication that therapists who are talkative and energetic have shorter therapies than therapists who are taciturn. Getting an estimate from the therapist as to how long the therapy will probably take not only helps you decide on a suitable time period for your agreement, but orients you to the work ahead.

Fees and Appointments   Hopefully, you will have established the therapist's or clinic's fees beforehand. If for any reason you have not, you will want to determine the fee right away and decide if it is a reasonable sum for you to pay.

You also need to think about the fee in relation to frequency of sessions. If the therapist feels that the number should be increased at a later point, this should be clarified from the start since it is important in determining whether it is economically feasible for you to pay for therapy under those conditions. What does the therapist consider the optimum number of weekly sessions for you to be? Does the therapist want to start once a week and then increase the frequency later? Will the therapist work with you on a once-a-week basis because that is all you can afford, even though he/she prefers to see you more frequently? Will the therapist want to increase the number of sessions if you can afford it at some later time?

There are no clear guidelines on how often sessions should be scheduled to produce the best results. As a generalization, the more ambitious the goals, the greater the change you desire, the more frequent the sessions should be. More frequent sessions permit greater intensity of feelings and thereby help to bring about significant change in you. Research suggests that clients who are so defensive that they find it hard to become involved in therapy on a once-a-week basis can make better progress if the session frequency is increased. There are important individual differences here; some clients move along faster in therapy on a once-a-week basis than others who go two or more times per week. There is also no clear relationship between the frequency of sessions and the total duration of the therapy process. While clients often expect that a greater frequency of sessions will mean they can finish the therapy sooner, it can happen instead that it prolongs the therapy because the additional visits allow the client to broaden out the original therapy goals. The limited research that is available suggests that once-a-week sessions are a necessary minimum for a meaningful psychotherapy process. Most therapists consider once a week a minimum for supportive therapy, and twice a week a minimum for therapy aimed at personality changes based on a deeper understanding of yourself.

Another issue concerning fees is the manner in which the therapist wants to be paid—at each session, weekly, or monthly. Does the therapist or clinic qualify under your insurance coverage? Will the therapist fill out your insurance forms? Will the therapist fill them out during sessions or at a different time? Will there be a charge for filling out your forms? Some clinics bill clients for preparing such statements.

What is the therapist's policy about sessions you miss? Will the therapist automatically bill you for all missed sessions? Will the therapist bill you for absences that are your choice (going on vacation) but not bill you for those that are unavoidable (being in the hospital)? If the therapist bills you for all missed sessions, will makeup sessions be offered? Therapist practices with regard to missed appointments vary widely, but there is less rigidity now about charging for missed sessions than there was in the past. Independent practitioners tend to be more amenable to arranging for makeups than therapists in clinics, who usually have to adhere more closely to standardized procedures. Theoretically "orthodox" practitioners are more apt to charge for missed sessions than adherents of the new approaches that have a greater spirit of flexibility built into them. While there is some rationale in consistently charging for missed sessions (see chapter 6, "Sore Spots"), a therapist who does so without offering makeups and regardless of the circumstances indicates a rigidity of attitude that may interfere with his/her ability to be sensitive to you.

What time is available for your appointments? Is this time convenient for you? Are alternate times available for makeup sessions, or is the offer to permit makeup sessions an empty gesture?

How long will your "hour" be? Most sessions are for a fixed time of 45 or 50 minutes, but a few therapists leave the time indeterminate and end the session whenever they choose to. There is no definitive research on the relative effectiveness of different length sessions. The 45-to-50-minute hour was settled into on an empirical basis, working out well for clients' needs and being a convenient way for therapists to divide up their time, allowing for a client every hour with a short break in between. Although there are occasions when a fixed time will not seem enough, or other occasions when it will seem too long, knowing the time allotted to you for each session helps you to use it more constructively. You can gauge yourself accordingly and, if you do not utilize your time to good advantage, it can make your resistance to working at therapy more apparent. Some clients use the time as a way of "testing" the therapist's concern for them. They will leave important material for the end of the session to manipulate the therapist into extending the time for them. Some clients feel "cut off" when the therapist announces the end of the session and interpret this as a sign of disinterest in them. If you recognize that the time has been prearranged, it will help you separate your concerns about the therapist's regard for you from the realities of your arrangement. Many clients leave it to the therapist to announce the end of the hour, seemingly oblivious to the amount of time they have left. It is one of the obligations of the client to the therapist to recognize the limits of the session and not to ask for more than what has been agreed upon.

One of the difficulties in making financial arrangements is the current unstable economic climate, which sometimes makes it questionable how long a client will be able to pay a particular fee and how long a therapist can continue to charge a particular fee. Although the financial part of your agreement may have been negotiated in good faith, changing conditions might make it impossible for either one of you to keep to its terms. Some therapists are willing to reduce their fees when a client runs into financial difficulties, such as a loss of job, but it is unreasonable to expect a therapist to work for an extended time at a fee considerably below the usual one. Although it is unfortunate, a client's inability to continue to pay for sessions may mean that the therapy relationship will have to end. Another problem occurs if the therapist wants to raise fees because of cost-of-living increases. It is also unreasonable to expect a therapist to keep the fee constant when his/her expenses go up markedly. If the probability of a fee increase looms on the horizon, it can be specified in advance that the agreement will be valid for only a limited period of time, at which point the fee may be renegotiated within limits that have been specified beforehand.

Availability of the Therapist   When starting out in therapy, clients take for granted that the therapist will be available for them as long as they want. This assumption often turns out to be false. Because of their training functions, clinics and psychotherapy centers have a large turnover of therapists. Many stay at a clinic for only one or two years to meet training requirements and then leave for other jobs or to start private practice. That makes it a good idea to check beforehand how long the therapist intends to remain on staff. Some therapists at clinics will be able to continue seeing a client after they leave for private practice. However, in such instances, the therapist may want a fee increase. Other therapists are bound by contractual agreement not to take clients with them when they leave.

Although private practitioners are more likely to be available for extended periods, they too move, accept part-time appointments, or change office locations, any of which can influence their availability to you. It is always wise to ask the therapist if he/she expects to remain at the same location for the foreseeable future and to have the same hours open for you. While no one can be expected to make firm commitments into the far future, some therapists might be planning changes of one sort or another that would affect you, but that they might not mention if you do not raise the question. For example, if you were to arrange for lunch-hour appointments that you can just squeeze in at the present office location, and the therapist is planning to move the office to the other side of town, you will not be able to continue therapy as planned. Similarly, if a therapist is contemplating a part-time teaching appointment and will no longer have your afternoon hours open, you should know about this in advance.

Also check on the therapist's vacation schedule. Some therapists take one to three months time off in the summer, which may be longer than you want to go without regular sessions.

It is also a good idea to ask about how often the therapist expects to cancel sessions because of other professional commitments. Some therapists like to give lectures at symposiums, therapy technique demonstrations or such, and they interrupt their regularly scheduled client appointments to meet these commitments. If this is acceptable to you, fine, but if not, you should inquire beforehand whether such interruptions are likely to occur.

Another aspect of availability, which becomes important if you are in a crisis situation when you enter therapy, is the amount of extra time the therapist has to see you at other than your specified sessions. Will the therapist try to see you on an emergency basis? Does the therapist feel it is more beneficial for therapy to hold tightly to the set schedule and thereby not to be available for extra sessions?

Will the therapist speak to you on the phone if you have a problem that you feel cannot wait for the next session? Telephone conversations can be a touchy issue between therapist and client. Some therapists will discuss crises on the phone but others feel the phone is an inappropriate medium for working on a problem. The rationale for these attitudes is discussed in chapter 6, "Sore Spots."

Termination   One of the areas to be clarified in advance is the conditions under which you, or the therapist, may terminate your agreement. If you feel that the therapy is not working out and that you are not making progress toward your goals, you should have the right to terminate the agreement. However, you have an obligation to notify the therapist beforehand and to discuss the basis of your dissatisfactions. What if the therapist feels the client is not working at the therapy and that it is fruitless to continue working with that person—does the therapist have the right to terminate after giving prior notice and discussing his/her dissatisfactions? If a therapist feels that the therapy is stymied, the question of termination should be brought up and discussed. But if the client still wants to continue therapy, the therapist has an obligation to try and continue working with the client and to give the client a reasonable time period in which to come to grips with the problem. Of course, if the client should not live up to his/her obligations, such as refusing to pay for services, the therapist has the right to terminate. Some therapists use the threat of termination as a way of making clients comply with new conditions. Having an agreement of specified duration and specified working arrangements makes it less likely that a therapist will try to threaten you in this way. However, if this should still happen, it is better that you terminate since such a coercive relationship will not be productive for you.

Confidentiality and Records

Professional ethics require the therapist to keep confidential all that transpires between you and him/her. Under no circumstances should a therapist provide any information about you, written or oral, without your written permission to do so. However, violations do occur so it is best not to take confidentiality for granted and to spell out guarantees in your agreement.

Most therapists feel free to present your "case" at professional meetings or in journal articles without requesting permission, provided that your name and other identifying data is deleted. However, it is up to you to determine whether any material about you may be presented and, if so, what details should be deleted to protect your anonymity. Sometimes others will request information about you from the therapist at your or their behest. You might, for example, ask your therapist to provide case history material to another professional in conjunction with a consultation, or an insurance company may request information about your therapy to determine if you qualify for reimbursement. If you do authorize a release, it should specify what information is to be provided and to whom. While most therapists will not send out such information without your authorization, many do not want to show you what they did transmit. They will rationalize their behavior, saying that you will be unable to understand the material properly, or that it might be harmful for you to see it at that particular time. It is arrogant for a therapist to assume that you are not "ready" to handle what he/she tells others about you. If there is any question about your ability to understand a communication, it behooves the therapist to explain it in a way that you can grasp.

It is common practice in clinics to discuss cases for supervisory and training purposes. This is usually in the client's as well as the therapist's interest. But you should know if and when your therapy is discussed and you might want to know with whom. As mentioned earlier, you also will want to find out who has access to your file. At clinics associated with hospitals, clients are sometimes asked to attend a case seminar where the staff members can see and hear the "case" in person. At these case presentations various people will feel free to question you and observe your reactions, but usually you will be invited to leave without getting the benefit of learning firsthand their impressions of you and your problems. You are under no compulsion to participate at such a seminar, and should not let yourself be pressured into doing so. If a therapist does try to pressure you to participate, he or she is putting personal interests above yours.

Sometimes therapists make tape recordings or take notes during sessions. These are often used for seminars, case presentations, research, or books. In such cases the tapes or notes are for the therapist's purposes rather than yours and it is up to you to decide if you want to allow it. Some therapists have taped sessions without the client's awareness. This should not be tolerated.

One aspect of confidentiality that is removed from the therapist's discretion is a situation in which information might be requested by a court in conjunction with legal proceedings. For example, a therapist might be asked to testify about your mental condition or moral character in reference to your competence to obtain or retain custody of a child or to administer estates. Another situation could be your accountability under law for criminal acts. The degree of protection offered you would depend on the extent to which the concept of privileged information is recognized for the profession of the particular therapist you see. Confidentiality accorded to psychologists is the broadest. It was explicitly defined to equal that of the legal profession and protect all communications between the psychologist and the client. Psychiatrists, who practice under the confidentiality provisions for physicians, cannot offer such broad protection. The confidentiality provisions for physicians state that the practitioner shall not communicate without the patient's permission any information relevant to the disorder for which the patient consulted the physician, but information not relevant to the disorder is not protected. Psychiatrists are trying to broaden this protection but the courts to date have not been willing to extend it.

A Formal Contract

Most contracts are in the nature of oral agreements, but a tendency seems to be under way toward more formal contracts. It has recently been suggested by the Washington-based Public Citizen's Health Research Group that the agreement between therapist and client should be specified in written form. The Health Research Group has developed a sample contract, which they offer for use as a model by all clients going into therapy. It includes the following major elements: the name of each party, the date of beginning and end of the agreement, the length of each session, the goals toward which the therapy will be directed, the cost of sessions and time of payment, the services to be provided by the therapist, provisions for terminating and canceling sessions, provisions for renegotiation of contract, provisions for changing therapy goals, acceptance of lack of guarantees for attaining therapy goals but statement of good faith, and access of client to records and client control of access by others.

There is a good deal of resistance among therapists to making formal contracts. The Health Research Group found this resistance stronger among psychiatrists than other practitioners, perhaps because it is contrary to the traditional doctor-patient relationship, which places all power in the doctor's hands. Regardless of professional identification, many therapists rely on the doctor role for their own sense of security and, therefore, are hesitant to accord their clients equal footing. Some therapists object to formal contracts because they see them as having a limiting influence on the therapy; others may fear greater susceptibility to malpractice charges or to legal suits. Still, it is important that you come to an understanding with the therapist, whether it is written or oral, formal or informal. If you find that you cannot make suitable arrangements for the course of the therapy relationship, there is very little hope that it will be a productive therapy.

6.
Sore Spots

ALTHOUGH YOUR ARRANGEMENTS WITH THE THERAPIST should be spelled out at the start, unforeseen situations do crop up later on, some of which can be quite bothersome. These problem areas generally stem from a lack of understanding on your part, and/or the therapist's part, of the rationale involved in various therapy arrangements.

Missed Sessions
One recurrent point of tension is the policy of charging for missed sessions. If you wake up late and miss a session, it is easy to see your responsibility in missing it and you probably won't mind paying for the session. But what if you break a leg and obviously can't get to the office because you're in traction? On top of your medical expenses, why should you have to pay the therapist when he/she knows you can't make it? Or suppose you were caught in a traffic jam, stuck in an elevator, or attending a funeral. Is the therapist right to charge you under such circumstances?

There probably isn't any one correct attitude toward the various situations that may arise, but it is important that you and the therapist are in basic accord on the issues involved. If you resent his/her approach, it will be a constant bone of contention between you and will hamper a productive relationship. Different attitudes toward money are not necessarily something that can be "worked through." Of course, it just might happen that you are the type of person who always has to have something to fight about, and having a therapist whom you can always accuse of greed might be a perfect situation as far as you and your problems are concerned. But more frequently, disagreements about payment reflect differences in basic attitudes that make for incompatibility.

When the issue of payment for missed sessions occurs, most clients automatically resent the idea that they should pay. Many agree to pay anyway just because they think this is the way it is in the field. A few admit some right of the therapist to charge them, but pay up resentfully, feeling that the therapist is more concerned about the fee than about them. Why should a therapist receive a fee for sessions when he/she does not work? In answering this question, clients generally use other professional situations as models, most frequently drawing an analogy between the therapist and physician or dentist.

What happens when you have an appointment with a physician? If you come on time, chances are you will be kept in the waiting room anywhere from a half-hour to an hour or more waiting for the physician who, invariably, was delayed at the hospital. The physician will see you when he/she has time, regardless of the time originally set for your appointment. If you call up to cancel an appointment, you are usually not charged. You did not really have a specific time reserved for you in the first place and if you do not show up it does not upset the physician's schedule. By contrast, your therapist keeps a specific hour open which is a time for you and no one else. You will not be kept waiting except, perhaps, once in a while for five minutes or so, in which case extra time will usually be added at the end of your session. If you call to cancel, your absence is decidedly marked. For the time of your appointment, your therapist sits in the office with no other clients going in and out of the door. Of course, he/she might use the time to make phone calls or read magazines, but the fact remains that a specific time has been set aside for you and you are not there to fill it.

The analogy to dentists is a little more apt, though still not quite up to the mark. Your dentist probably will set aside a certain time for you and, if you should cancel, be left sterilizing the instruments or making phone calls. Dentists often do charge a cancellation fee but, more importantly, clients are very unlikely to cancel dental appointments, wanting to get them over with quickly. In fact, a dental appointment is the type of situation for which clients are tempted to cancel psychotherapy appointments. Psychotherapy appointments are ongoing and experienced with less urgency; if a client misses a therapy session, he/she is often content to wait for the next regularly scheduled session. When a person cancels a dental appointment, he/she usually wants to schedule an alternate time right away. Another difference between the dental and psychotherapy situations is that dentists are more likely to fill canceled sessions with other clients, while a psychotherapist's canceled session can rarely be put to remunerative use.

When we look at therapy as an educative process, and take schools and tuition payment as a model, the parallels seem much closer. If you sign up for a course you know that the class will meet x times a week, and that you pay full tuition regardless of whether you miss any classes or not. If, for any reason, you miss a class, you work harder to make up for lost time. So it is in therapy. Your therapist signs on with you for a course to open up your ways of thinking and experiencing. Class meets regularly once or twice a week, or however frequently specified, and is open for you to attend whether you can make it or not. The time is reserved for you, and if you do not show up it is lost both for you and the therapist. Just as a private tutor or school will bill you for a stipulated number of lessons whether or not you attend, psychotherapists also expect to be paid for prearranged time.

Although there is a good rationale for the practice of paying fees for missed sessions, there is little need for adhering to this practice rigidly. Some therapists make strict rules to avoid misunderstandings and the hassles that result from these, others because they do not take clients' needs into account. It is important that clients recognize their obligation to pay for scheduled sessions, but it is also reasonable to provide some flexibility for canceling or changing sessions. The client and therapist should discuss the conditions under which a session can be canceled without the client being charged for it. Some therapists apply a "twenty-four-hour notice" rule, and bill for all sessions canceled without such prior notification, regardless of the reason the client does not come.

This policy recognizes that even though a client may cancel for unavoidable reasons, the therapist should not bear the burden for the client. The client's obligation to respect the therapist's time is not reduced by such situations. When notice to cancel is given earlier than twenty-four hours before the session, the reasons for such cancellation become relevant to the decision about billing. If a client cancels for unavoidable reasons, and the therapist can arrange a makeup session, there is little rationale for charging. But if cancellations are made irresponsibly, there is little rationale not to charge. Financial obligation for missed sessions also helps to reduce habitual cancellations that stem from resistance.

It is important that there is reciprocity between therapist and client about rights in canceling sessions. For example, if the therapist wants to be free to cancel sessions to attend professional meetings, he/she should respect the client's right to cancel for reasons of comparable importance. The therapist should not assume prerogatives that he/she is not willing to accord to the client.

A frequent practice is to offer a makeup session when a client cancels for an unavoidable reason such as illness or an important business meeting. While the therapist's desire to maintain income may be part of the reason for the prevalence of this practice, there are others that relate to the therapy itself. If sessions are not made up, there can be an interruption in the flow of the therapy, which hampers progress. This can be especially pronounced when the therapy sessions are scheduled less frequently as, for example, once a week, where a two-week lapse between sessions can create a break in the process. Another important reason for a makeup session is to preclude an uncommitted attitude toward therapy. But when the therapist insists on making up a session missed by the client, the therapist should also be prepared to offer makeup sessions when he/she cancels the session. When the therapist cancels, the client has a right to know why the therapist is canceling.

Some therapists do not charge for canceled sessions if they can fill the time with another client. The rationale for this practice is solely income protection for the therapist. It leaves the client with a sense of uncertainty, not knowing beforehand if he/she has to pay and having to rely entirely on the therapist's honesty.

Schedule Changes

Once you have arranged your therapy hours, both you and the therapist expect that they will be maintained. However, something might happen that makes it impossible for you to keep that schedule—a change in jobs gets you off work too late or cuts into your lunch-hour appointment, you have to be home earlier because your kids get out of school earlier, or whatever. Under such circumstances, you will want to work out more convenient hours, but the therapist may not be able to accommodate you. This does not necessarily mean that the therapist is rigid, unconcerned, or spiteful. Usually, changing your hours means changing someone else's hours as well and a therapist is not free to offer you new times if his/her other clients are unable or unwilling to change their schedules. For the same reason, you may find your therapist asking you one day if you can switch your appointments around. Sometimes clients resent being asked to make changes, feeling they are being put out to accommodate someone else. Of course, you do not have to make a change or inconvenience yourself, but you might want to help someone out if you can. Other clients may try to accommodate themselves to you in the future, although they are no more bound to do so than you are.

Therapists may also ask you to switch your appointments around to accommodate themselves. Many therapists have part-time teaching appointments or consultantships that change from year to year. The therapist has an obligation to check with you beforehand about your schedule rather than just expecting you to make changes to meet his/her needs. When asking you to make a change the therapist should tell you the reasons for it. He/she should not try to intimidate you into altering your schedule or threaten to terminate if you cannot arrange new times.

A related problem is the timing of individual sessions. Sometimes a therapist may run overtime with a previous client and keep you waiting. This can anger clients who feel they are being used for another's convenience—which is so. Clients tend to be touchy about this when they are concerned that the therapist does not really care about them, or if they think the therapist likes other clients more. If a therapist keeps you waiting, the lost time is usually made up at the end of your session. If this is not convenient for you because you have to race off to another appointment or back to work, the therapist should make up the lost time when it is convenient for you. The therapist should not presume on your time and make a habit of keeping you waiting and extending your appointment. Occasional incursions may be warranted, just as your time may run over into someone else's, but if this becomes a pattern, the therapist is being inconsiderate and treating his/her time as more valuable than yours.

The therapist is not the only one who is late for sessions. Sometimes clients show up late too. Habitual lateness is often a sign of resistance, anger toward the therapist, or a way of testing the therapist, but people can be late for a variety of reasons beyond their control: traffic tie-up, accident, and so on. When you show up late for a session, regardless of the reason, the situation is analogous to your missing a session without notice. No matter how unforeseen the circumstances, you cannot expect the therapist to have time to extend your session accordingly. It is an unfortunate happenstance of life, which may occasionally befall you as it does the therapist and other people.

Vacations

Therapists generally encourage clients to take vacations when they do. This creates less disruption in the therapy process and in the therapist's practice. Many therapists charge for clients' vacation time if it is taken outside of the therapist's vacation. Some have even charged for whole summers if the client was away, for example, to study in a foreign country. The practice of charging for vacations originated when summer was the usual time for taking vacations. Therapists worked for the duration of the school year, from September to June, July, or August, and expected their clients to conform to this schedule. With the changes in vacation patterns brought on by the jet age, including the popularity of winter, spring, and autumn vacations, it has become less realistic for therapists to expect clients to take their vacations only in summer months. Although there is good reason for clients to try to coordinate their vacation schedule with the therapist's, for a therapist to insist on this is to ignore the legitimate needs of the client to take a vacation when it is best for him/her to do so. If we grant the client as much right as the therapist to take a vacation when he/she wants, there seems to be no justification in billing for vacation time that falls outside the therapist's vacation schedule. The right of the client to take a vacation without paying for missed sessions should not be abused to the point of the client's taking off for excessive amounts of time. The client is entitled to "separate but equal" vacation time.

Naturally the client has the right to be away from the therapy for an extended period of time, but not with the expectation that the therapist must be available on the same terms afterward. The therapist cannot be expected to guarantee the time for a client who chooses to interrupt the therapy unless the client reserves that time by paying for it.

Phone Calls and Emergencies

There may be times when you want to talk to your therapist before your next session because you feel especially bad or because of a crisis that has come up. Even if the therapist is willing to arrange an earlier session, you feel you just cannot wait till then and have to get some help right away. Do you have the right to call the therapist? Does the therapist have a right to cut you short under such circumstances?

If your need is urgent, then by all means call. The therapist should discuss urgent problems with you on the phone, though not all therapists will agree with this. Some will object on theoretical grounds, considering such phone calls as an indulgence in feelings that should be contained. Others feel that since they are paid on the basis of time, telephone calls constitute an abuse of their services. This could be a consideration if a client makes a habit out of such calls, but most clients call rarely and do so only if they have no other recourse.

It can happen that clients use telephone calls and crisis situations as a way to test the therapist's concern for them. In such cases the problem, although real, is usually not so critical that it cannot wait for a day or two. A client may know this, but call anyway just to see how the therapist reacts or to get reassurance that the problem is not that catastrophic. It is a good idea, if you want to phone, to ask yourself first if you really need help or just want to test out the therapist.

Though a therapist should be available to discuss a crisis over the phone, the client has to recognize that the phone may be an inappropriate medium in such a situation. Phone calls can help, but they are not a replacement for direct personal communication. A therapist might be reluctant to talk with you at length over the phone and insist instead that you come for a session. If the therapist is willing to make time available for you outside of his/her normal working hours, the additional session is usually offered in your interests rather than as an excuse for cutting short phone contact.

You will have to indicate just how urgent your need is and not cry "wolf." But if the therapist is not there for you at a critical moment, you may need a new therapist.

Phone Calls from Others

A frequent source of annoyance for clients is the therapist's taking phone calls during a session. Since the client is, in effect, buying a certain amount of time, there is justification for being annoyed at any encroachments on that time, but the realities of life sometimes necessitate interruptions. The therapist, like anyone else, needs to be available by phone not only because of those infrequent professional emergency situations but for personal emergencies as well. Granted the legitimacy of telephone accessibility, the therapist should nonetheless keep calls brief and, whenever possible, cut the call short and phone back on his/her own time.

The annoyance of interruptions can be lessened by expressing it and by making up the lost time. Many therapists overlook these time losses, making their clients rightfully more angry. It often happens, though, that clients will be angry even when the therapist does make up the time because they resent other people or other problems intruding into their sessions. While this is an understandable reaction, it is an unreasonable demand. On the other hand, the therapist should recognize that a crisis of the client during the session is every bit as pressing as one that may be coming in on the telephone line and be prepared to let the phone go unanswered when the disruptions would be harmful to the client. The incoming call, as well as the client in session, may have to wait at certain times.

Smoking

Some therapists object to clients smoking on the ground that it allays anxieties that otherwise could be profitably worked on during a session. Some therapists feel that clients should relieve their discomfort by smoking if they so wish. Others feel that clients should be dissuaded from smoking during sessions as well as at other times because it is a health hazard. Still other therapists personally dislike smoking and want clients to refrain from it in sessions.

Many therapists tend to forget that clients may also have feelings about the therapist smoking. Nonsmokers may resent being subjected to the smoke created by therapists, and smokers as well as nonsmokers may be bothered by excessive smoking as a sign of lack of control on the therapist's part. If the therapist's smoking bothers you, you have a right to ask the therapist not to smoke; he/she should be able to go for forty-five to fifty minutes without a cigarette.

If either the client or therapist has strong feelings about smoking, that should be discussed at the start. The therapist has a right to set his/her conditions and you have a right to accept or reject them, as well as vice versa. Hopefully, smoking will not be an issue on which you and the therapist cannot accommodate each other. In light of the harmful effects of smoking, it is prudent to favor the needs of the nonsmoker.

Note-Taking and Recording

Many therapists take notes or tape-record sessions. Some ask for the client's permission and others take it for granted. If you have feelings about your therapist taking notes or recording your sessions, be sure to discuss them. The therapist does not have the right to take your consent for granted. Some clients feel that it is a violation of their privacy and others find it distracting or disruptive of the interaction. Still others feel that it shows a lack of concern on the part of the therapist in that he/she cannot remember the important things unless they are written down or taped. Note-taking and tape-recording can serve a variety of purposes and the therapist should clarify what these are. Records to enable the therapist to keep track of your work together are in both your interests. Records for research, seminars, case presentations, or books are in the therapist's interest. If the therapist needs notes to keep on top of the process or for record keeping, the therapist should not let the note-taking intrude on the interaction but should do it on his/her own time. If the therapist keeps notes or records for his/her own purposes, there is little reason for you to put up with it if it disturbs you.

What to Call Each Other

The way you and the therapist address each other says a lot about the kind of relationship you have. Usually client and therapist start off addressing each other formally by last name, with the client using the therapist's professional title, if any. Many therapists want the formality and prestige of being called by their title. After working together for a while, therapists usually start to call clients by their first name. This informality arises naturally for therapists out of the personal contact they have with their clients. It is not disrespectful unless the therapist uses the more familiar first name without a corresponding feeling of closeness to the person. Then it represents a condescending familiarity and will be experienced as a put-down.

Some therapists start right off on a first name basis to undercut the social distance implied in using last names, inviting clients to call them by first name, too. Occasionally clients will start off calling the therapist by his/her first name on their own initiative, but for most that form of familiarity does not express a genuine feeling of closeness. Most clients see their therapist as an authority figure and feel more comfortable using his/her last name (or avoiding using a name altogether) until such a time as they can experience the relationship on a more equal level. Some therapists always call clients by their last names, even after years of work together. Considering today's informal customs, clients can also become resentful of this if they feel it shows a lack of warmth. The therapist may be too reserved or bound to the professional role to become more personal.

Sometimes a therapist wants to be addressed by title and

last name while calling clients by first name. The disparity can arouse a lot of bad feeling. Any person, therapists included, can ask to be addressed formally, but then that person has the obligation to address others on the same level. If a therapist thinks it is proper to call you by a first name there is no justification for insisting that he/she be called by last name and title.

Small Talk

Usually both the client and therapist enjoy a bit of personal banter. Such encounters are a pleasant diversion and helpful in getting to know each other. It is natural to be interested in each other: where are you going on vacation, how did you like the ballet last night, did you read about so and so in the news, et cetera. The danger comes if such exchanges begin to revolve more and more around topics of exclusive interest to the therapist. For example, a therapist may, in asking about how you enjoyed your vacation, get carried away and start asking for various details about the trip, the scenery, the hotels, the restaurants. Or the therapist may pursue his/her interest in hot tips from a business client, or for political gossip from a journalist client, or for the "dirt" on the social set. Clients tend to go along and answer questions because they are anxious to please the therapist, or because it keeps them from having to get back to work. But after a while they will become resentful if the therapist is using their time in a way that is not productive for them. They may feel the therapist should not ask irrelevant questions during the session, although they would be glad to answer such questions afterward—when they are usually not asked. It is unfortunate if a therapist lets his/her interests intrude into your session in this way, and it is even more unfortunate if you allow this to continue. If you need to curb the therapist too much, the question arises as to whose needs are being served by the therapy.

Changing Techniques

A therapist may, seemingly out of the blue, ask you to make a change in your way of working together. He/she may want you to switch from the chair to the couch, to join a therapy group, to do body exercises, or to go on a weekend marathon. A suggestion like that might be made because the therapist feels that it has become appropriate at that particular point in your therapy, because he/she has just become acquainted with or trained in that technique, or because he/she now feels free to ask you without your kicking up a fuss. Whatever the reason, the change has to be agreeable to you. Discuss the reasons the change is being suggested, air whatever questions or doubts you have about it, and then see how you feel about it. You may, after discussion, think it's a great idea, you may be skeptical but willing to give it a whirl, or you may be completely turned off to the idea. Whatever your reaction, it is your decision whether or not to go along with any changes in therapy that were not agreed upon at the outset of therapy.

Avoiding Questions

Often clients want to know how the therapist feels about a particular issue, his/her reactions to experiences brought up, or something about the therapist him/herself. These may be questions such as "What is your attitude to abortion?" "How do you feel about my decision not to go home?" or "Have you ever been married?" As discussed before (in chapter 3, "How to Pick a Therapist"), many therapists avoid answering questions like these even though they are relevant to the therapy process. Such questions are often turned against the client, with the implication that there is something wrong about asking them.

Some therapists avoid answering these questions on the assumption that it is detrimental to the therapy. They think that the more neutral the therapist remains, the more the client will reveal about him/herself. Being important figures in a client's life, therapists are bound to be influential even without wanting to be so. But these considerations do not make it necessary for a therapist to hide his/her attitudes or to pretend a neutral stance. When you want to know how a therapist feels about any issue, you have a right to bring up the question. Of course you must explore the reasons why you want to know: Do you have doubts about what you are doing and need reassurance, are you afraid the therapist might not approve of what you are doing, or do you want to check your own attitudes against those of someone you trust and respect? Once you know what is at stake for you in determining the therapist's attitudes, and once you have examined your own attitudes on that subject, there is little reason why the therapist should feel constrained about telling you how he/she feels. In fact, it can be very helpful for you to learn how to deal with attitudes of important others that may diverge from yours, without suspending your own judgment.

Besides questions about attitudes, clients also ask therapists questions for clarification and explanation: "Do you see anything else in that dream?" "Why do I feel so anxious?" "Why did you ask me that?" Many therapists also avoid answering these questions on the grounds that doing so allows the client to shirk his/her own therapeutic work. Sometimes clients use questions in this way, and then it is best for the therapist to delay answering to encourage the client to take the initiative. Nevertheless, therapists have a responsibility to answer client questions as well as to point out the client's passivity.

Social Interaction

As client and therapist work together and develop closer feelings toward each other, clients sometimes want to extend the relationship outside of the office. Frequently, clients want their therapists to come to events marking a milestone in their life, especially since they are often related to work done in therapy. For example, the therapist may be invited to the client's wedding, to the opening of the new shop or the client's art show. Sometimes therapists are invited to other personal occasions such as a cocktail party or dinner. Is it all right to invite your therapist and is there any good reason why he/she should not accept?

Despite your friendly and warm feelings toward each other, the psychotherapy relationship is not the same as a friendship. First of all, it is not a mutual relationship. In therapy, the client's needs are always uppermost and the therapist has the responsibility to defer to them. Friendships are built on greater mutuality, on freer give and take. Friendships also differ in that they are multifaceted, whereas therapy relationships are primarily oriented toward the client's problems and growth. The therapist, because of the nature of the relationship and needs of the client, is subject to restraints and formal commitments that do not exist in friendships. To have friendlike social contact with clients, the therapist has to step in and out of roles and for this reason many prefer to stick to the therapist role, at least until the therapy is terminated.

Therapists will accept or reject your invitations depending on their conception of their role as therapist, their flexibility in dealing with different roles, their feelings about you and how important the events are to you, and their own attitudes about the particular event. A therapist should accept your invitation only if he/she really wants to attend, but may sometimes reject an invitation even if he/she wants to attend. You should extend an invitation only if you really want the therapist to come. Some clients feel obligated to invite their therapists to important occasions and others invite them only as a test. Often clients feel uncomfortable when their therapist does accept the invitation because the therapist's presence makes the client self-conscious and ill at ease. Invite your therapist if you genuinely want him/her there, but also be prepared to discuss your reasons for the invitation as well as the therapist's reasons for accepting or declining it.

Similar issues arise in connection with asking for favors from the therapist—letters of reference, letters of excuse, the loan of a book, and so forth. While the therapist must keep your needs uppermost within the therapy situation, this obligation does not extend to matters outside of it. Clients generally feel rejected if the therapist does not want to go along with the request, but a refusal is sometimes appropriate and not always a rejection. Of course, the therapist should discuss his/her reasons for refusal with you if he/she cannot go along.

7.
Making Therapy Work

WHAT ACTUALLY HAPPENS IN THERAPY? WHAT DO YOU
do, what does the therapist do? According to the old stereotype,
all you have to do is talk and the therapist listens. But a lot
more goes on in therapy than that. True, you will have to do a
lot of talking since you—your feelings, your attitudes, and
your problems in living—are what the therapy is all about.
The burden rests on you to make yourself known as fully as
possible by providing the material for you and the therapist to
work on. That work, however, is a constant interchange of
effort, a constant back and forth.

The therapy sessions usually start with you bringing up
something you want to talk about. This can be anything that's
on your mind at the time: an argument you had with the bus
driver coming to therapy, a dream you had last night, feelings about your mother, or something left unresolved from the
last session. Often sessions center on current problems, and
talking about them provides relief as well as bringing out
underlying therapeutic issues. Whatever you talk about, your
job is to be as honest and straightforward as you can be. Try
not to hold back any thoughts or feelings because of embarrassment; you have to let your feelings out to learn to accept them and become a whole person.

The therapist's job is to help you express yourself by providing you with a relationship that allows you to open up and
experience the threatening feelings you block off. He/she
exposes you to new routes to awareness—free association,
dream interpretation, role playing, body exercises, and other

techniques—and helps you use them to get in touch with yourself. The therapist doesn't just sit there but listens and observes carefully to help you discover what he/she learns and utilize this knowledge to overcome the barriers you experience. By mirroring back what you say or how you say it, he/she can make you aware of aspects of yourself that ordinarily slip by you. The therapist calls your attention to feelings and attitudes that may be emotionally loaded by emphasizing them when you gloss over them. He/she notes sudden changes in your behavior ("You became so animated talking about your father. What were you feeling then?") and helps you examine inconsistencies in your behavior that suggest conflict ("Last time you were so optimistic but today you seem down in the mouth. What is going on?"). The therapist helps you grasp connections between your feelings and behavior ("Look how tightly your hands are clenched—you started clenching them when you started talking about your mother"). The therapist also makes you more aware by calling your attention to what you don't do or don't say ("Last week all you talked about was your upcoming interview with your boss, but today you haven't said a word about it. I wonder why"). Through the supportive interaction with the therapist, through dialogues and confrontations, you will learn new ways of experiencing, be exposed to new perspectives, and encouraged to try out new alternatives in responding to life's problems.

Clients often think that explanations of their behavior will be the answer to their problems. This idea makes it difficult to understand why the therapist makes them work at developing insights on their own when seemingly he/she has the answer all along. Insight alone is not enough; it is a precondition for changing your feelings and behavior. Moreover, insight cannot be given to you but has to be actively acquired. The lack of insight does not stem from insufficient knowledge but from emotional forces that resist that knowledge. Only through a change in your readiness to face that knowledge, an increase in your confidence that you can take it, can the insight occur. While the therapist can lead you to that knowledge and encourage you, it will become meaningful only through your active acceptance.

Things that are hard to face are usually accepted only gradually. Acceptance comes about by repeatedly going over the same issue, though often from different perspectives, to build up the tolerance and courage to act on it. This process, called "working through," is often a difficult aspect of therapy and the point at which many people want to quit. They become disillusioned that the initial insight did not lead to change and that the major job of doing something about themselves still lies ahead.

Therapy is bound to be a bumpy road with times of fast movement, times of no progress, and times of plateaus. Undoubtedly you will feel antagonistic to the therapy at times. Being prepared for these feelings and knowing what to do in therapy is the best antidote for times of discouragement. Approach therapy as openly as possible and work with those techniques that seem the most natural to you.

Talking

Psychotherapy has been called the "talking cure," and talking is still the basic component of most psychotherapies. As a process of exploration into oneself, only you, the client, can provide the material. It is up to you to present as much information as possible, to lay open the thoughts, fears, expectations, fantasies, anxieties, and feelings that constitute your existence. To do this, talking is usually the most direct approach. Talking is not only a medium of communication but a help in and of itself. It stimulates thinking, evokes feelings, and allays anxieties. Often in the process of verbalizing feelings and identifying them one learns how to deal with them more productively. Talking is the point at which psychotherapy begins, the way in which problems will be expressed, goals set, and the conditions arranged for the therapeutic relationship.

The beginning sessions of psychotherapy are usually tinged with anxiety about starting out and finding the right therapist but, in another sense, these sessions are easier because there are clear issues to bring up. After the first few sessions, in which the major problems and reasons for seeking therapy are outlined, some clients suddenly find that they don't know what to talk about. Should they go into detail about their childhood histories, talk about anything that comes into their heads, or sit back and wait for the therapist to ask questions?

The course you take may be influenced by the psychotherapy approach and practitioner you have chosen. Some therapists will be more directive, some less so. Some will want to concentrate on childhood and some on contemporary events, and some will want to observe what you will do. Still, there are some guidelines you can follow in bringing up material.

Talk about what seems most meaningful to you at the time. If several issues are pressing all at once, the particular one you pick is not all that important. The goal is to develop deeper understanding of your way of living. This awareness can come through talking about anything and everything that matters to you.

Try to talk about yourself in a direct rather than indirect third-person way. The more concretely you talk about your experiences, the more alive you can make them in the sessions, the greater the possibilities of understanding what is going on. For example, instead of summarizing your reactions to generalized situations ("When I am at large gatherings I feel insecure"), talk about what it was actually like when you were in such a situation ("When I went to the party I got this terrible feeling in my stomach and felt I would throw up every time someone spoke to me").

Try to talk about events in your life in terms of how you, not others, experience them. Instead of focusing on the reactions of others ("When I had lunch with my mother she thought the food was awful and the service was dreadful and she didn't enjoy it at all"), relate your reactions ("When I had lunch with my mother she made me feel bad because she was critical of everything that was happening and I had the feeling she wanted to put me down").

Try to talk about things as what they are rather than as what they are not. For example, "I feel like crying" rather than "I am not happy," or "I feel I could kill you" rather than "I do not want to talk to you."

Try to talk about your feelings in a situation, not just the details of what happened to you. For example, instead of talking about events happening around you ("My boss came in and told me I would have to prepare a whole new report that night to be ready for the nine A.M. meeting"), talk about how you feel when these things happen ("When my boss came in and told me what I would have to do, I got so angry I could feel my face getting hot, but I just couldn't get any answer out of my throat").

Try to say things as you think them. Do not polish up your thoughts for the therapist or put them into polite language or quiet tones. Let them come out as you experience them. For example let the therapist know that "When you sit there looking so goddam smug, I could punch you in the nose," rather than telling him/her that "You have such an odd look on your face."

Try to be as open as possible and let your thoughts and feelings emerge even if they are embarrassing or shameful to you. If those are the feelings that are hanging you up, those are the feelings you must deal with. The more you express them the less hold they will have over you, and the less horrible they will seem.

If you feel "stuck" and at a loss for words, try then to describe that experience as well. "I don't know what to talk about. My mind is a blank. It makes me feel so uncomfortable. You must find me so dull." If you get too upset in a session, the therapist is there to help you. "I just feel awful. Say something to me."

Past or Present

Reconstructing events of the past can be, but is not always, an important element of therapy. There is some magical belief that if you can only recall your childhood you will find the clue to contemporary problems, which will then fade away. It is not the events in themselves that are important, but the meaning extracted from these events. The past is important insofar as it gives rise to certain attitudes about yourself and your possibilities in life. When these attitudes become set and are not changed by present experiences, understanding the past can help you understand your present reactions.

Some clients want to deal only with current issues and

resist attempts to focus on the past. People interested in the "here and now" may feel it is a waste of time to bother with the "there and then." A refusal to look at past events or feelings about early figures in one's life sometimes masks a defensive posture and fear of stirring up painful echoes. Or it can be akin to the demand for "relevance" of the last student generation in its attempts to throw history out of the curriculum and replace it with contemporary social studies. Relevance cannot be determined in a vacuum: one must first get an overview before deciding what is meaningful and what is not. But when a client feels that such an endeavor has out- lived its usefulness, there is no point in continuing such a course just because the therapist wants to fill in the gaps. Covering the past, if done as an automatic exercise, can become a waste of time and divert therapeutic energies from more meaningful pursuits.

Holding On to Your Thoughts

Sometimes clients in therapy want to bring up all sorts of thoughts, memories, or feelings at their next therapy session only to find, when they get there, that they have forgotten everything but the memory of having something to talk about. This happens when you have "resistance" to bringing up certain material in the therapy sessions, or when the anxiety around the thought is so great it becomes uncomfortable to keep it in mind. Thoughts also get lost naturally when your mind is occupied with other aspects of daily living. Having to remember things to do for the job, or what to buy for supper, or letters to write, can take your attention away from the seemingly less pressing problems of your inner self.

There are some simple ways to help you keep track of those thoughts which pop in and out of your head. One is to keep a pad on you and to jot down thoughts or memories you don't want to lose. Just the act of putting them on paper tends to make them stick more, but once they are written down you do not have to rely on your memory. Some people find it helpful to keep a diary when they start therapy for much the same reason. They can go over the day's events and cull from it feelings and experiences that were especially meaningful. A diary can also help you in the process of self-analysis, if it is used not only as a record of events but as a distillation of the experiences as well.

Silence

Some people cannot tolerate silence. When they are alone they use the radio or television to fill in the emptiness with sound. When they are with another person silence can also be difficult to bear if it is assumed that people should always be talking to each other. When this assumption is applied to the psychotherapy situation, silence becomes discomforting because it is experienced as awkwardness or a waste of time and money. Does silence in a psychotherapy session mean that the therapy is getting nowhere, or can it also be useful?

Silence, like talk, can be used both constructively and destructively. The value of the silence will depend on how you experience and use it. Silence is necessary to search for or reflect on memories, ideas, or feelings. Sometimes silence follows an outpouring of emotions, where time is needed to integrate the feelings that have just been experienced. Therapists will generally not interrupt a period of silence if they think you are using that time to experience yourself more deeply.

Sometimes therapists ask clients to be silent for a while because too much talking can be a way of occupying time with irrelevant material. If there are uncomfortable issues to discuss, or feelings that cause embarrassment, excessive talking can be a way of avoiding coming to grips with these feelings. If the therapist senses that you are using talk as a defense against opening up, he/she might ask you to be silent to rid your mind of smoke screens that are keeping you from coming closer to what is really bothering you.

Silence can also indicate a lack of communication between you and the therapist. If you feel uncomfortable or angry with the therapist, you are more apt to clam up and feel further resentment if he/she does not attempt to break through the silence. Often the client sits waiting for the therapist to speak or to inquire as to the meaning of the silence. In part, it is up to the therapist to sense the quality of the silence and the purpose to which it is being put. However, if you are not talking because of discomfort with the therapist based on his/her insensitivity to you, the task of breaking that silence falls on your shoulders.

Therapists have been accused of using silence as a retreat of their own. Clients sometimes feel, especially if they are not face to face with the therapist, that the therapist is unconcerned when silent or using that time to daydream. This can very well be the case. If so, there will usually be other signs of therapist disinterest in you as well, such as lack of attention to what you are saying or inability to remember important facts about you. More often than not, an inexperienced therapist will talk too much rather than too little. The neophyte therapist can also be uncomfortable with silent phases, fearing that they reflect his/her inadequacy as a therapist rather than a legitimate space for experiencing on the part of the client.

Free Association

Freud's "basic rule" in psychoanalysis was that the client must say everything that comes into his/her head no matter how trivial, unpleasant, or irrelevant it seemed. This process is known as free association. Rather than trying to relate thoughts in an organized way, the client was instructed just to let thoughts and feelings come as they would and to be "absolutely honest" in reporting everything that came to mind. Freud likened free association to looking through a railway window and reporting to a fellow passenger the changing views outside.

The idea behind free association is that if you follow the spontaneous trend of your thoughts and feelings rather than try to organize them consciously, sooner or later important feelings and memories that have been blocked off will surface, providing the material for therapy. A client may, for example, ramble on in an associative stream about movies seen, popcorn eaten, gum wrappers on the floor, disgust with fellow movie patrons, anger at society and its filth, annoyance with spouse for making the house dirty, and a memory from youth of coming home to a filthy house presided over by a sloppily attired mother. In the preceding stream of thought, it eventually becomes apparent that the client feels hostility toward the spouse and mother and that he/she finds it difficult to confront the issue directly. Evoking such thoughts, in addition to creating awareness of repressed feelings, helps to discharge unpleasant emotions in the process.

While orthodox Freudian therapists still use free association as the basic tool, the technique does not have primacy among therapists of other persuasions. People are psychologically more sophisticated than they were in Freud's day and more capable of zeroing in on their problems. Many therapists view free association as a process that consumes unnecessary time, and some feel that the associations are often detached journalistic recountings, which do not have enough emotional impact for the client. What matters is not just the relating of all thoughts and memories but the reexperiencing of these memories in an emotionally meaningful way. Free association is not always genuinely free and clients can hide their feelings behind an associative stream of sterile facts and details. Since most clients enter therapy because they are in some way blocked off from their feelings, they cannot engage in genuine free association. It is only after they have made some therapeutic progress that they are truly able to free associate and reexperience the emotions that have been blocked off.

A lot of clients today prefer to focus on their problems directly and to use free association when they are blocked and have run out of things to say. While it is difficult to free associate in a genuine way at the outset of therapy, using the technique does encourage you to open up pathways to hidden feelings and to recapture the immediacy of past experiences. If you feel that you have run dry of things to talk about or that you have already covered everything and all that is left is to repeat yourself, you might productively try free association. If, however, you find that the process is not suited to you, if you find yourself unable to let thoughts and feeling flow in a genuine way, do not force yourself into such a process on a prolonged basis.

The Couch versus the Chair

The couch, originally introduced by Freud as an aid to the free association process, has become an integral part of the psychoanalytic mystique. Reducing stimulation from without by reclining in a room with subdued light fosters the flow of ideas and feelings from within. To the extent that the therapy is modeled after the psychoanalytic process and geared to a full exploration of your feelings, the couch can be a potentially useful tool. However, if your therapy is geared more to specific and immediate problems, you will probably find it easier to work on them sitting up. As a gestural process, sitting up conveys a stance of active engagement. It is a posture in which you are accustomed to think and communicate. Lying down is a passive stance associated with dreaming, fantasizing, and letting oneself be engulfed by more basic feeling processes. The posture you assume should suit the type of process your therapy is aimed at eliciting.

Since many psychotherapists practice both problem oriented and "uncovering" psychotherapy, many offices are equipped with both chair and couch. On entering an office clients sometimes assume that they are supposed to use the couch and occasionally a therapist will propose it, but that is not an appropriate way to start off. In the initial sessions it is more suitable to sit up facing the therapist. Once your goals and ways of working together are defined, the issue of couch versus chair will more naturally settle itself. If a therapist should insist that you use one or the other, and you are uncomfortable with that choice, feel free to talk about it and state your preference. While the couch can be helpful in the associative process, there is no magic in the couch and you should not feel coerced into using it.

Dreams

Dreams have long been recognized as representing a unique aspect of human awareness and dream interpretation has figured importantly in many ancient cultures. Freud, who regarded dreams as the "royal road to the unconscious," helped to reintroduce the modern world to the psychological significance of dreams and made dream interpretation a cornerstone of psychoanalytic technique. The dream is an intense experience in which the dreamer is open only to those phenomena corresponding to his/her present mood and feelings. Accordingly, the dream engages the dreamer in a vivid and concentrated way. In therapy, dreams can help point to areas of emotional difficulties that are unclear or avoided during the waking state, and thus broaden the client's awareness of his/her way of being in the world. While potentially of great therapeutic value, the usefulness of dream interpretations varies with the client's ability to be open to dreams and the therapist's ability to help analyze them meaningfully.

When people start therapy, they are often unaware of having any dreams. Since research has indicated that people dream all the time, the lack of dreams seems to relate to the inability to recall them in a waking state. If you are unaware of having dreams or forget your dreams between the time of waking and the therapy session, you can probably get yourself into the habit of remembering them. When you go to bed, tell yourself that you would like to dream and when you do wake up from a dream think about it right away to let it get ingrained in your mind before drowsing off again. Keeping a pad near the bed to jot down notes on the dream as you awaken will help. Some people even keep a tape recorder near the bed and repeat the dream onto the tape as soon as they wake up. After you play it back to yourself, you will find it easier to remember the dream.

Tell your dreams to your therapist as you would any other experience. Try to recapture the feeling tone of the dream: how you felt in the dream, if and when your feelings changed, and how you felt as you woke up from the dream. You can then try to relate the feelings you experienced to the activities and situations within the dream. You can also associate to the various elements in the dream. What do the dream situations remind you of, and what do the particular dream objects—schoolroom, hotel, lake, people, or whatever—remind you of? If the people are unfamiliar, do any memories come to you as you think about them? If they are familiar, what were the situations in which you knew them and what are your feelings about them? Sometimes reconstructing what happened on the day of the dream helps capture its meaning: what did you do, what feelings did you have, and are those feelings or events somehow related to the dream? When you have prepared yourself with this additional material, going over the dream again may help in understanding its meaning. Given this input from you and your associations to the dream, the therapist can help you analyze it by adding his/her perceptions and associations.

Dreams, like everything else in life, have meanings on

different levels. Therefore, dream contents can be interpreted correctly in different ways. For example, suppose a person dreams after starting therapy that he is at the movies watching a film. That dream might be reflecting the dreamer's interest in observing his own life now that he has entered into therapy, or the way the dreamer lives his life—usually outside of activities, partaking of life as a passive observer—or the dreamer's feeling of not being directly in touch with people but coming into contact with people who are playing roles rather than with real people. Any one of these interpretations might be correct, or all of them together. To get the most out of a dream, don't stop analyzing it as soon as you have an insight; look for meaning on as many levels as possible.

There are as many different theories about dreams as there are theories about psychotherapy. According to Freud and his followers, dreams express the unconscious wishes of the dreamer that he/she cannot own up to in a waking state. The dreamer, alert to the possibility of this forbidden material breaking through, "censors" the dream so that the final dream product is a statement of the repressed wish in disguised form. The actual dream (its "manifest content") is a distorted statement of the actual wish ("the latent content"). To understand the dream, one must cut through the distortions and discover the true latent meaning. In this approach to interpretation, it is possible for the dream analyst to turn the dream content on its head, since every dream symbol is assumed to be a disguise. For instance, in a dream reported by Theodor Reik in *Listening with the Third Ear,* a patient who dreamed of being afraid of a dog was, according to Reik, actually afraid of God: Reik reasoned that dog spelled backward is God and, thereby, that the dreamer did not want to recognize his repressed impulses, which were contrary to his religious beliefs. Non-Freudians dismiss such an interpretation as doing an injustice to the dream and base the interpretation on the meaning of the dog to the dreamer, rather than assuming that the dog is merely a disguise for something else. Following such a line of thinking, the therapist might say that the dreamer was afraid of his animallike instincts, which are one and the same as his fear of the dog. It is possible that the dreamer's animal instincts are not in accord with his or her religious beliefs, but the dream deals fundamentally with the fear of animality, not with the fear of God.

Freudian dream theory allows the therapist to impose interpretations on the client. If it is assumed that the dream contents are a distortion of unacceptable wishes, then the therapist becomes the authority, since the dreamer is not privy to the real meaning of the dream. If the dreamer does not accept the interpretation, it is taken as a sign of resistance. In such a situation, the client is often reduced to going along with a therapist's interpretation even if it does not make sense to him/her.

Some therapists have a way of introjecting themselves into their clients' dreams by interpreting important dream figures as themselves in disguise. Because clients do not always feel free to acknowledge their feelings about the therapist, therapists often look for hidden signs of clients' involvement with them in dreams. If a client has a dream about a teacher it is possible, of course, that the dream is making a statement not only about the teacher but about the therapist insofar as he/she is also teacherlike. But it also happens that therapists see themselves in dreams with little justification. The following dream interpretations, from Walter Bonime's *The Clinical Use of Dreams,* illustrates this tendency. The client had been working on her fears of the therapist's becoming really friendly with her, since it was so difficult for her to relate to people. At one session she reported acting inappropriately with people, being silly, destructive, and behaving "like an ass." As she said this she recalled a dream: she is in a nice house set in a park, but inhabited by a crazy woman —wild and unreasonable. The crazy woman is very hostile to her. The client wants to stay but is afraid of the crazy woman. The therapist's interpretation of the dream was that the crazy woman was himself because the client was afraid of accepting him as a friend and because his office was on Park Avenue—the park in the dream. Bonime overlooked that the memory of the dream was triggered off by the client's recognition that she is destructive and acts "like an ass." She acts, in fact, much like the crazy woman in the dream. If the focus is put on what the client is feeling, it becomes more reasonable to interpret the crazy woman as representing the crazy part of the client, her silly destructive ways, of which she is becoming aware but cannot yet break from. The house seems to be the client's house, where she would like to live if she could make peace with the silly part of herself who also lives there. Assuming it is the therapist's house because he lives on Park Avenue ignores that a park has little relationship to the strip of concrete known as Park Avenue. To insert himself into the dream, the therapist forces the dream contents to fit his interpretation and loses track of what the client is saying about herself.

A recurring point of difficulty for clients is stereotyped sexual interpretations of dreams. Objects with elongated shapes, snakes, tall buildings, pencils, rifles, and so on, are assumed by many therapists to be phallic symbols when they occur in dreams. The dreamer is then seen as making some statement of penis envy, fear of castration, or something pertaining to phallic strivings. Similarly, receptaclelike dream objects such as pocketbooks, bathtubs, sugar bowls, are assumed to be symbols of the vagina and again expressive of the dreamer's sexual desire. While snakes, buildings and rifles do bear some structural similarity to each other and to a penis, such an approach to dream material avoids the question of why one dreamer dreams of the penis, another of the snake, another of the building, and still another of the rifle. A snake is like a penis in that it is made of living tissue, but a building is a lifeless edifice, while a rifle is not only lifeless but life-negating. It is in the actual meaning of the dream contents that the richness of the dream is unfolded, rather than in automatic mechanical interpretations. An approach to dreams that views them as straightforward statements, though in a different symbolic language of images rather than words, is apt to provide interpretations that are more valid and acceptable to the client.

An important guideline in working with dreams is that the interpretation must make sense to you. Do not accept a therapist's interpretation as valid just on his/her say-so. It must not only be meaningful to the therapist, but meaningful to you. If you feel uneasy about an interpretation because it misses the point or does not seem true to your feelings, accepting it on the therapist's authority is doing yourself a disservice.

Therapeutic Exercises and Strategies

A whole host of exercises and therapeutic strategies, originally developed as therapy technique systems in and of themselves, have become incorporated into the more traditional psychotherapies as adjuncts to the basic talking process. These techniques have been borrowed from psychodrama, Gestalt therapy, behavior modification, and other systems with the idea that, although not sufficient in and of themselves, they are useful in broadening out awareness or in providing clients with immediate help in coping with various problem situations.

Role playing is a widely used technique and practiced in many variations as an aid in helping clients deal with persons and situations that are perplexing or anxiety provoking. For example, if a woman client feels she is being exploited by her husband but is afraid to tell him off, she might role play this situation, with the therapist taking the part of the husband. By engaging the client in this interaction in as realistic a way as possible, the therapist brings the client closer to experiencing what is causing her anxiety and she gains the opportunity to practice ways of dealing with it. One variation of this technique is role reversal, in which the client takes the role of the other person with the therapist taking the role of the client. To follow through on the above example, the wife would take her husband's part and the therapist the wife's. In this situation, the client can experience how her behavior triggers responses in her husband and she can learn alternate approaches to her husband from the therapist's behavior. Role playing facilitates coming to grips with anticipated situations by putting the client in closer touch with the feelings aroused in both parties and by offering an opportunity to explore and practice various modes of behavior. A Gestalt therapy variation on role playing has the client enact conflicting roles or aspects of him/herself. The client, playing out the "top dog" part of him/herself—the bullying self-righteous conscience—sits in one chair yelling at that other part of him/herself in the empty chair to "shape up" or "do better." The client then switches to the other, "underdog" chair to play out his/her submissive but tricky self who defies the top-dog aspect: "Please, give me another chance, you don't let me live!" In this way the client discharges stored-up feelings and becomes aware of his/her inner conflicts.

Exercises have been designed to heighten awareness of many common problem areas. For instance, some exercises are specifically directed at developing assertiveness. By letting the client behave in a dramatically assertive way, these exercises enable him/her to experience directly both the bodily and emotional components of this mode of behavior. In a typical exercise, the client stands up, feet apart, and says in firm clear tones, "Me," while striking the chest. Clients who have difficulty in self-assertion initially find such an exercise embarrassing and difficult to do, but while doing it they gradually become comfortable and build up competence in this behavior. As such exercises become spontaneous, the client at the same time assimilates the experience of self-assertion. In a similar way, other exercises direct themselves to particular trouble spots. Some try to help the client release stored-up feelings of anger. The client beats on a pillow more and more vigorously while giving vent to the angry feeling: "I hate you, I hate you." Although the activity may seem artificial at the outset, when it is continued the client becomes emotionally engaged and the experience can become very real. The exercise not only lets out anger but helps clients lose their fears of their own aggressive feelings. Other exercises are directed at developing feelings of trust. The client, with his/her back to the therapist, falls backward into the therapist's arms. In this situation, the client's feelings of trust or distrust for the therapist are very clearly experienced, and practicing "letting go" in the fall at the same time affirms the client's ability to trust the therapist.

Another group of exercises tries to broaden the client's awareness both of the world of objects and of him/herself as a physical being. An awareness exercise might direct the client to make up sentences stating what he/she is aware of at a particular moment as, for example, "Now I am aware of . . . how the words on this page stare up at me." "At this moment I am aware of . . . the itchiness of the chair covering." Some exercises focus on sharpening the client's contact with the environment. The client shifts attention from one object to another, noticing and verbalizing emotions: "I like this but not that part of it," "I don't like that," "This I hate." A body awareness exercise might have the client lie down with eyes closed and focus on the sensations of the body: How does the body feel, what are the points of tension, how can the body shift and reduce the tension? While becoming aware of bodily sensations such as "a pain in my neck" or "a weight on my chest," the client also tries to become aware of the intertwined feelings: "Who is giving me a pain in the neck? What is weighing me down?" and so forth. Other body exercises direct the client to emotional awareness of different body postures. Clients take various positions—submissive, assertive, angry, aggressive, et cetera—and direct their awareness to the feelings these bodily expressions evoke. Or, the client can be directed to focus on a particular function of the body: "Feel yourself breathing. Feel the air going into your nose, down through your windpipe, into your lungs. Feel the rib cage expand, the chest expand. Feel the muscles relaxing, the breath exhaling." Breathing exercises are also frequently utilized as a means of relaxing and of controlling anxiety.

Imagination exercises focus on areas of insecurity or conflict. They require the client to imagine being in such situations and to try to capture the feelings. For example, the client might be instructed to imagine swimming nude in a pool with his/her father. The therapist then asks, "How would you feel, what would you say, what would your father say?" Or the client is asked to imagine standing next to his/her father. "Lean over and whisper something in your father's ear. What did you say? How do you feel? What does he reply?" In guided fantasy exercises, the therapist leads the client in the fantasy by offering supports along the way. "Are you frightened, do you want someone with you, would you like to go on, can you do it by yourself?" When the client has successfully grappled with the problems in the fantasy and no longer feels troubled, the therapist lets the client leave the fantasy situation.

Behavior therapy techniques can also be incorporated into the therapy to help clients overcome problems involving either their own habits or interpersonal situations. For example, if one of your problems is running short on time and being disorganized or unable to accomplish all that you feel you should, you can try to work out, with the therapist's help, a reasonable schedule of tasks to set yourself in a given period of time. Or, if one of your problems involves money, you might try working out a reasonable budget for a certain period of time. In the process of working on the practical aspects of a problem you might also find yourself becoming more able to come to grips with its emotional aspects. As you make entries into your budget or cross tasks off on your schedule, you can also try to focus on the feelings involved in doing so: how does it make you feel when you are spending more money than you should, and when you are spending what you consider reasonable? Similar processes can be worked out with problems involving another person. For example, when two people who live together irritate each other in little ways, each person can draw up a list of behaviors disliked in the other, and the list can be used as the basis of a compromise. Disliked behaviors can be "traded off" against each other. Tallies can be kept of the disliked behavior, and appropriate "penalties" charged against the offender—such as contributing an extra dollar to the joint account or washing the dishes twice in a row. These devices, while not getting at the root of the problem, can help to allay undue distress while therapy works at trying to deal with the source.

Some techniques are more in the nature of therapist strategies to evoke feelings and awareness in the client. One technique is for the therapist to mirror back the client's behavior in an exaggerated way—to highlight certain aspects of a client's behavior. For example, if a client is stuck in the feeling that he/she has no alternatives but to do the bidding of others and complains "I have so little time for me because I have to take care of Jim, meet my mother at the airport, balance the bank statement, et cetera, et cetera," the therapist might repeat these statements while assuming the martyr position of a person on a cross. Such caricatures of client behavior can convey to the client an immediate awareness of what he/she is doing, although there is a risk that this can be done in a mocking fashion. Another strategy for the therapist is to unexpectedly agree with the client when he/she expresses attitudes that are basically untrue but which he/she is unwilling to relinquish. While the client is prone to repeat these attitudes to him/herself and to others, their falsity can become apparent when they are expressed about the client by someone else. For example, a client who hides behind an attitude of inferiority may tell the therapist, "I know why I wasn't invited to the party. I'm really kind of boring and I don't have much to offer. The others are so much brighter, they've been around, they're scintillating, but I'm dullsville." When the therapist agrees with the client, "You're right. Why should they want you at the party—you're dull and uninteresting while the others are scintillating and exciting," the client, in anger at this characterization, may be able to detach him/herself from such self-defeating attitudes.

Therapists vary in their inclination and skill in utilizing available techniques. If your therapist tries to engage you in any, it is a good idea to be open and experimental and see which of these exercises and strategies you can work with. You might find all of them helpful, some of them, or none of them. If suited to your temperament, the various exercises can help the therapy to progress at a more rapid pace. Most clients have found, however, that while these can get you out of a rut or push you along, they are not a substitute for talking and working through.

Using the Interaction

Your therapy sessions are not just for reporting on other events. They are a live interaction that will provide much of the material for therapy (as discussed in chapter 8, on "Feelings About the Therapist"). As you work with the therapist, you are going to have feelings about what the therapist says, does, or asks. You will find yourself feeling pleased, annoyed, hurt, admired, or rejected. You will find yourself wondering, "What does he/she think of me?" "Why is he/she so quiet?" "What is he/she thinking now?" Or you might ask yourself, "How come he/she ended the session so abruptly?" "Why does he/she always interrupt me when the time is up even when I'm in the middle of a sentence?"

Whatever your feelings and regardless of whether they seem irrational, embarrassing, or insignificant, do not keep them bottled up inside. How you react to the therapist and what you do with your feelings are as much a part of you as the way you behave on the outside. Although you will probably find it difficult at first, learn to use your sessions to discuss what is going on between you when that is where your feelings are at. The therapist is another person in your life with whom you want to establish a relationship that is meaningful to you, and you have to be able to work it out with the therapist as well as with anybody else. Indeed, the therapist should provide the atmosphere that facilitates your being able to express yourself spontaneously: to confront, to question, to complain, to appreciate, to admire, to love.

Groups

It is not uncommon for therapists to ask their clients to join a therapy group after they have been in individual psychotherapy for a while, and some even make joining a group a precondition for working together. Other therapists who have clients in group therapy also see them individually, but that is not always the case. Sometimes a therapist will see clients in a group who are seen individually by another therapist. As with other issues in therapy, there are no hard and fast rules that apply to everyone, and whether or not a group situation is suitable for you must be evaluated by you.

If your therapist asks you to join a group, find out first in what ways the therapist thinks it will be helpful. If the idea of a group appeals to you and the rationale is sensible, by all means join. If, however, the idea of a group turns you off, sounds nonsensical, or frightens you, the issue should be explored further. Discuss any doubts or reservations you might have rather than join just on the therapist's say-so.

Some of the fears about groups center on the expectation that the group members will gang up on the new members and rip them to shreds. Unfortunately, enough people have been exposed to destructive group "therapy" encounters for this possibility not to be taken lightly. Part of the value of the group experience is that it encourages people to express themselves openly. As a result, group members are frequently rewarded by peer approval when they do let themselves go and let their feelings "hang out." In such a climate, the hanging out of angry feelings is just as appropriate as the hanging out of feelings of anguish and despair. In fact, the greater "vibrancy" of angry feelings over feelings of desolation some-times gives the former the appearance of being more "basic" and the group may therefore tend to encourage the expression of hostility more than other emotions. Because of this, unas-sertive people can get hurt in a group if it is not carefully guided in the interests of all. Most therapy groups, however, have a positive orientation, with members who are more in-terested in giving each other mutual support than in tearing each other down. If you are starting in a new group, the others will be in the same boat and probably as fearful as you. If you are entering an ongoing group, most members will remember their first session and initiate you with consideration and awareness of your hesitant feelings.

Of course, some of the fears of joining a group reflect the individual's own fears of being with others in a more open situation. To the extent that this constitutes the core of the resistance to joining a group, the group should be beneficial in that it provides an opportunity to work directly on that fear.

An important aspect of the group is the types of people in it. Before entering a group, you have a right to know some-thing about the others who are going to be in it. Some thera-pists think this is irrelevant and interpret such an interest as a manifestation of resistance. It is, nonetheless, a very relevant factor because you will get more out of the group if you are compatible with the participants. A good group is usually a varied group, but one varied in terms of sex, marital status, field of work, or interest, rather than in terms of values and basic outlook on life. It is important that you feel you are not "out of tune" with the group. The nature of the group interac-tion, the level of psychological sophistication, and the group goals should be appropriate to you. If you are a single person, or recently separated, you will not find it useful to work in a group with others who think preserving marriage is the highest calling in life. Your time in the group should not be spent fighting the others but working with each other, and whatever facilitates supportive interaction is going to make for a productive group experience. If you feel that a group is condescending because you are the only one without a college education, it does not necessarily follow that you have to stay and work this feeling through. It could very well be that it is a snobbish group and you should not burden yourself with it when you could get more out of a group experience with other people. Similarly, if you feel that the other group members are unsophisticated and insensitive, this does not mean that you are a snob. It may indicate instead that you would benefit more from a group experience in which the other members were more tuned in to you and your way of thinking.

If you are critical of the group, ask yourself if your criticisms are valid or defensive. You might not get much help from the group in evaluating your feelings because the group exerts pressure on its members to belong. The therapist will probably ask you to express your criticisms to the group, and you should do that if you possibly can. But if you can't confront the group, do not let your difficulty in asserting yourself keep you bound to a group that is not useful to you.

Certain group sizes work better than others. General experience suggests that a group of less than six persons is not apt to be very effective, that a group of around eight is optimal, and that a group of more than ten is cumbersome. Because the number of persons in a group is important, therapists sometimes try to push clients into joining a group to maintain a minimum core. Sometimes therapists will put together a small group in the hope of enlarging it. Don't agree to join a group in the expectation that it will shortly grow because it very well may not, and be equally careful that you are not being coerced into joining a group in order to swell the numbers. If you and the therapist agree on the desirability of your joining a group and your therapist does not have an ongoing group available, there may be alternate groups run by other therapists that you can enter. The group experience does not necessarily have to be with the same therapist. By the same token, if you are in a group that starts to shrink and you and the other group members feel that there are not enough participants, you are not bound to continue attending the group. When the group is no longer productive it should be disbanded. The therapist should suggest the dissolution of the group when it begins to fizzle, but if he/she is negligent in this respect the group members have to bring up the issue of dissolution themselves.

Groups make use of many of the same techniques used in

individual therapy. Talk is still a basic process, although a group setting particularly lends itself to such techniques as role playing and assertiveness exercises. The same general approach holds for group as for individual therapy: be as open and as honest as you can and express things as you experience them.

Getting Advice

Clients are often unsure whether or not they should ask their therapists for advice on problems in life such as splitting up a relationship, getting married, leaving or taking a job. Since many clients come to therapy because they have difficulty making decisions, the temptation to ask for advice is great. The uncertainty is often compounded by the variety of therapist responses: some are eager to give advice, some do it reluctantly, and some refuse to give it altogether.

If one of your problems is that it is difficult for you to make decisions, that's certainly an area you want to work on. Psychotherapy can help you discover and work through the feelings that hinder your making decisions, but your ability to make them is undermined whenever the therapist makes a decision for you. That does not mean the therapist cannot help you in the decision-making process. He/she can help expand your awareness of what's at stake in the decision, help clarify the possibilities, and support you in facing the consequences of whatever decision you do make.

A common area in which people have difficulty making decisions is commitment to relationships. For example, a man or woman may be involved in a relationship in which the partner wants to get married. The client finds it impossible to make a decision to marry or to separate: he/she has real doubts about the potentials of the relationship, but there is also much anxiety about living alone or the ability to form a new relationship. Overwhelmed by the conflict or the fear of living with the consequences of either outcome, the client wants the therapist to make the decision for him/her. In so doing, the client is asking that the therapist take the responsibility for making the choice. What the client needs is not a decision, but encouragement to take the risks involved in making one. Once the decision has been made, the client can, of course, expect continued support from the therapist in carrying through and meeting the consequences.

Making Changes While in Therapy

You may want to, or have to, make some major changes in your life while you are in therapy. Some therapists discourage their clients from doing so, fearing that feelings stirred up in therapy that may still be unresolved will influence the change that is made. While this possibility should always be considered, life cannot be held in abeyance because you are in therapy. You have probably undertaken therapy to help you lead a more productive life; to stop living and remain static is not the way to find fulfillment. On the other hand, just because you are in therapy does not mean you should force changes on yourself. Sometimes people feel that it is a good idea to make a major change earlier than they might have just because they are in therapy on the grounds that if the move does not work out they have support in dealing with the consequences. Major changes, whether in or out of therapy, should be made with sufficient time, if possible, to weigh the alternatives and to assess the feelings involved. Changing your life-style while in therapy should be helpful rather than harmful since the therapist can help clarify your feelings and weigh different possibilities.

Adjusting the Frequency

As was discussed (in chapter 5, "The Therapy Agreement"), there might be times when you want to increase or decrease the frequency of your therapy sessions. If you started off therapy tentatively on a once-a-week basis, you may find that this spacing of sessions does not allow you to get into things deeply enough and that your sessions are over before you have even begun to say what you wanted to say. You may find that such limited visits worked out fine in the past but now that you have gotten into a particularly troubling aspect of your feelings you need more frequent contacts to work them through. Or you might want to increase the number of sessions if you are going through a particularly difficult period caused by external stress such as a death in the family, the loss of a job, a serious health problem, or some other crisis. You may also want to increase your therapy sessions for less sound reasons. The desire for more frequent contact can actually be a desire to have the therapist take over and care for you more. Similarly, the therapist might want you to come more often to fulfill his/her needs rather than yours—becoming closer, making you more dependent, or augmenting his/her income.

Decreasing the frequency of sessions may also be called for at times. If you increased your sessions to work on a particular crisis it will probably make sense to fall back into the usual tempo once the crisis is resolved. Sometimes practical issues such as a change in your work schedule or financial circumstances require you to reduce your sessions. Sometimes people decrease the frequency of sessions when they feel more capable of handling problems on their own as a prelude to termination. On the negative side, decreasing the frequency may be a way of expressing anger at the therapist. You may think of coming less often if you are upset with the therapist and do not want to deal with these feelings. That is a way of giving the therapist a "slap" while at the same time protecting you from "having it out." Similarly, a therapist may suggest reducing the frequency of sessions because he/she is angry with you. The idea of reducing sessions may occur to both of you when you feel that the therapy is getting nowhere as a way out of looking at the real problem.

Because increasing and decreasing the frequency of sessions can be in your best interests or your worst, it is important that any desire to do so, whether emanating from you or the therapist, be carefully examined before it is accepted as a change in your contract.

Reassessing Your Goals

Clients and therapists are usually conscientious about setting goals at the start of therapy but inclined to forget about them soon after. As you get involved in therapy, you will probably find yourself a very interesting subject and may also find it easy to go far afield from your original objectives. Your digression may not become apparent unless you and the therapist periodically assess where you are at. Every so often, at intervals you can stipulate, but probably at least once a year in a long-term process, you and the therapist can sum up what you have accomplished and what still remains to be done in light of your original goals.

It may, of course, be perfectly sensible to change your goals as a result of what you have learned or accomplished in therapy. You may want to set your sights higher, direct them to more specific goals, or just reaffirm the original goals. For instance, a former goal of "speaking up against my mother" might be expanded to "being able to say what I think no matter who I'm with." Or a vaguer goal such as "overcoming the blues" may become more specific to "indulging myself without feeling guilty." But when you change your goals, it should be a conscious process and not just something into which you drifted. The more you and the therapist are aware of and convinced about the merit of what you are working toward, the better you will both be able to work. Having clear objectives helps to keep therapy from becoming an interminable affair.

Talking and Reading About Therapy

Some therapists advise their clients not to talk about the therapy with anyone other than themselves. The idea behind this is that feelings might get watered down or attitudes changed by discussing them with others, making them less available for exploration in therapy. While there is merit in the position that it is always best to express your feelings directly to the person involved, a policy of restricting your freedom to talk about therapy outside of the office represents a danger in its exclusivity. It also reflects a bit of grandiosity on the part of the therapist and contempt of you if it implies that other people are incapable of helping you to resolve these issues and that you will be unable or unwilling to bring them up once they have been talked over with someone else. Your therapy relationship must be open for inspection as much as any other relationship in your life. Of course, talking to others should not be a substitute for, or avoidance of, dealing directly with the therapist. Even though the therapist-client interaction is the core of the process, psychotherapy is not limited to the office and anything that helps you to expand your awareness is beneficial and should be encouraged.

It is very important that you let the therapist know what you do say about the therapy to others. This is not so that he/she can keep tabs on you, but to make sure that you do not avoid bringing up your feelings about therapy with the therapist. If you do, then something is wrong. The therapist may be intimidating you, or you may be angry at the therapist and trying to make him/her feel bad by not sharing important feelings with him/her that you do with others, or perhaps there are other reasons. Although you should feel free to discuss your problems with whomever you want, you must examine what is going on if your therapist is one of the people with whom you don't want to talk about your problems.

Sometimes therapists don't want you to talk about any issues with others that you should discuss with the therapist, such as unresolved feelings involved in decisions, dreams, et cetera. You might want to talk about these things because your sessions have not given you enough opportunity to explore your feelings or because you value someone else's views. Again, talking out feelings with others can dilute your experiences in therapy sessions, but the stricture to save these discussions for the therapist is not necessarily in your best interests.

Some therapists not only have an injunction against talking about your therapy with others but also against reading about therapy while you are in therapy. This injunction is based on the possibility that reading might confuse you, suggest things to you that are incorrect, or make you become too intellectualized in therapy. Though these possibilities exist, this attitude shows very little respect for you because it concludes that the overall effect of your getting additional knowledge will be more harmful than useful.

When you are in therapy you might be stimulated more than ever to read about therapy and learn all that you can about it. The more you read, the more you know, and the more possibilities you expose yourself to, the better. If your reading raises questions or brings up doubts, that's useful too. Therapy, of all endeavors, should not teach you to avoid life because life may create trouble.

Phases in Therapy

Typical therapy experiences are made up of different phases and changing moods. At the beginning of therapy, if you've made a good choice, you usually feel relieved. You have gotten over the initial hurdle of finding a therapist and are now with someone who gives you a willing ear on which to unburden yourself. Very likely you will get immediate help from the therapist in overcoming some of the most pressing difficulties you face at the time. But, as the therapy goes along, you start to realize that progress is not so quick or simple as you had hoped. The therapist doesn't seem to do anything concrete for you to make the problems go away. You begin to realize that you have a big job to do and that it is going to be tedious work. At times you will make progress and feel elated, but much of the time you will find yourself unable to move forward, and will feel discouraged. Sometimes you may even have the feeling of being worse off than before. This happens when problems and troublesome feelings you successfully warded off before begin to emerge in therapy. As you open up to these feelings they often seem to rush at you in an onslaught and make you panicky about your ability to control them. Even if you do not go through periods of disorganization brought on by a lowering of your defenses, you may become more disillusioned with the way you are. The status quo will no longer be acceptable to you because being in therapy makes you expect more of yourself and more out of life.

One of the more difficult aspects of therapy to accept is that progress is so unsteady. You wish for a constant rate of improvement and growth but instead find a hilly road with ups, downs, and long level stretches. Working hard does not always yield immediate payoffs, and finding out what is causing a problem does not mean that you are going to be able to shake it off. You will find yourself going over the same material again and again but each reworking, while seemingly repetitious, gives you the opportunity to develop new perspectives until problems gradually dissolve.

The ups and downs in therapy will be easier for you to live with if you have realistic expectations of what therapy is like. Typically, progress leads to anticipation of rapid changes, which is inevitably followed by disappointment. Change comes in spurts and patches, and sometimes coalesces when you least expect it.

8.
Feelings About
the Therapist

SINCE THERAPY INVOLVES YOU IN A CLOSE RELATIONSHIP
with the therapist it is likely that you will develop strong feelings about him/her. These feelings become as much a part of
therapy as the other feelings you bring in from the outside.
Recognizing and understanding them is a key element of
therapy.

Positive feelings toward the therapist are a precondition
for success. Unless you feel good about the therapist you will
not be able to open up fully and feel safe in revealing yourself.
Once the therapist demonstrates that your trust in him/her is
warranted, your positive feelings will be reinforced. But your
feelings are more than a barometer of client-therapist match:
they can be the crux of therapy. The more you tune in to your
feelings as you experience them in the interaction, the more
alive you are in the therapy situation; and the more you engage
emotionally, the better able you and the therapist will be to
come to know you as you really are. How you react when you
are with the therapist is as much a reflection of your personality as are your feelings and reactions to others. By being open
to the emotional interchange between you and the therapist,
you will learn as much, if not more, about yourself as you will
by exploring your feelings in other situations. Your encounters
with others can only be explored secondhand in therapy, but
your encounter with the therapist is immediate and potentially
of greater value.

The therapeutic relationship is structured in a way that
facilitates your coming in touch with and expressing feelings.

Compared to other close relationships, the therapy relationship is unique in that it is not based on mutuality of obligations. In therapy the client's emotional needs always come first and constitute the prime focus of the relationship. This creates a sheltered situation in which you can more safely express yourself. Being free from fear of rebuke and from having to deal with the therapist's needs gives you the space you need to experience yourself the way you really are. It is easier for you to let yourself feel anger if you do not have to worry about the therapist's counterhostility, or for you to feel tenderness if you do not have to worry about the therapist's taking advantage of it. The therapy relationship has been compared to the parent-child relationship in that both are concerned with creating an environment for growth aimed at helping the individual become autonomous. However, parent-child relationships are fraught with hidden agendas, with the parent's acceptance of the child only too often based on the child's ability to satisfy the parent's needs. The therapist, in contrast, must be prepared to make an unconditional commitment to the client and respect the client for who he/she is and is striving to become. Of course therapists, like other people, are rarely perfect, and it is unreasonable to expect that any therapist will always be able to keep his/her own needs in check and maintain that affectionate detachment necessary for good therapy. This is one reason a constant examination of your feelings toward the therapist and the therapist's feelings toward you is so essential.

Clients often say that the therapy relationship is not a "real" one. This is true in the sense that the therapist's professional role limits his/her personal involvement in order to protect the client from feeling impelled to respond to the therapist's needs. Nevertheless, the therapy relationship is real in the sense of two people having genuine feelings about each other that grow out of what takes place between them.

Therapy systems differ in their understanding of the nature and role of client-therapist feelings, but all agree on their importance. Freud used the word "transference" to describe the feelings of the client for the therapist. It was his belief that people carry around unresolved feelings toward early adult figures in their lives that are then transferred onto other important people. Thus the client relates to the therapist as if the therapist were the mother or the father, and examining the transference feelings enables the client and therapist to gain insight into the client's feelings about the parents. Sullivan introduced the term "parataxic distortion" to explain the feelings of the client for the therapist: the client distorts his/her perceptions of the therapist and others based on inappropriate generalizations from prior interpersonal experiences, with early experiences serving to mold the way people are perceived in later life. The existentialists maintain that the client-therapist relationship is a genuine relationship, not a transference phenomenon, even though distorted ways of perceiving may limit the manner in which the client can relate to the therapist. The way your therapist understands the nature of your feelings about him/her is going to have an important influence on the therapy process. If the therapist thinks that your feelings are only reenactments of past feelings toward your parents, the therapist is not going to be inclined to examine his/her role in bringing out certain feelings in you. If the therapist recognizes that you are engaged in a genuine relationship with him/her, even though you may tend to distort, the therapist will be more willing to acknowledge personal responsibility for bringing out reactions in you. While there is a tendency to perceive others in terms of one's preconceptions, people also react to the realities of the situation and may accurately perceive a therapist to be aloof, loving, or hostile, not because of one's mother, but because of the therapist. It is important to keep in mind that a tendency to misperceive your therapist's behavior and attitude toward you does not mean you cannot also make correct perceptions. Your feelings about the therapist will be a product of both the attitudes you bring in and the attitudes your therapist presents.

Typical Feelings About the Therapist

Because of elements common to all therapy relationships, clients' feelings about their therapists tend to fall into certain patterns. During the early stages of therapy, assuming you have made a good choice of therapist, you will probably be very impressed with your therapist. While you came in confused, the therapist seems to be very clearheaded and insightful. He/she may quickly be able to highlight things that have been bothering you for ages and help you put your problems in a new perspective. You become impressed with how knowing your therapist is, and assign an omniscience to the therapist that he/she does not possess. Because the therapist has been able to broaden your understanding, it is easy to believe, and you will want to believe, that the therapist knows everything and can help you with everything. The more faith you have in this idealized therapist whom you are creating, the more optimistic you will feel about the therapy. You may start to fantasize that the therapist is a perfect person. If he/she is so knowing about people, his/her personal life must run smoothly and everything the therapist does must be wonderful. Unfortunately, few people are so perfect but, even more unfortunately, many therapists find it necessary to maintain your admiration of them in this way and try to encourage rather than clarify such distortions on your part. It is necessary that you respect and like your therapist, but the therapist's ability to help you understand yourself does not make him/her a superbeing. Also remember that reliance on the wisdom and expertise of a marvelous therapist is not the road to success: it is not the therapist's understanding of you that is important but the therapist's ability to help you understand yourself that matters.

The tendency to idealize the therapist also makes it natural for you to want the reassurance of knowing that this wonderful person admires you. Do not be surprised if you find yourself courting the attentions of your therapist and trying to get him/her to take a more personal interest in you. If, for example, you have started to take more care dressing whenever you have a psychotherapy appointment, or you arrive a little earlier for your sessions, it may be that you want the therapist to take more notice of you. Perhaps your interests take a slightly different turn than they did before and, surprisingly, in the direction where you think the therapist's interests lie. If the therapist has his/her own paintings on the wall, perhaps lately you have been talking in your sessions of all those art shows you want to visit. Or maybe you have been tracking down the therapist's publications and talking about them in your sessions. It is also possible that you, like many others, will start feeling sexual interest in the therapist that you want to have reciprocated. Knowing that the therapist finds you sexually attractive is a way of knowing that you are admired. If the therapist does not respond to you with the admiration and interest you want, you may find yourself feeling hurt or rejected, and come to experience the therapist as cold and aloof. You may even start to wonder why you ever thought this uncaring person was so nice. Whatever feelings do occur, try to look at them in the perspective of your situation. Knowing that it is not unusual to feel rejected under these circumstances will help you to sort out whether your feelings are coming from unrealistic expectations or from truly callous behavior on the part of the therapist.

Unrealistic admiration of the therapist can lead to negative feelings in other ways as well. Often, when the client has built the therapist up into some godlike figure, he/she is bound to feel betrayed when the therapist turns out to be less than divine. If you do not expect perfection and the therapist does not pretend to it, you will both be better able to recognize and deal with therapist shortcomings if and when they intrude.

The exclusive focus on client needs in therapy facilitates wishful fantasies about the therapist. Because the therapist is always there for the client and does not withdraw acceptance, some clients imagine that they have found the idealized parent or lover. They try to use the therapy relationship as a substitute for other, less "perfect" relationships and become disappointed, perhaps even angry, when the therapist does not make their fantasies come true. Therapy cannot replace the missing relationships in one's life, but understanding the need to use therapy in this way can help to make possible more meaningful relations with others.

Idiosyncratic Feelings About the Therapist
To the extent that we all have idiosyncratic ways of looking at the world and experiencing events and people, you will find yourself looking at your therapist from a very personal perspective as well as from a typical client perspective. This perspective is influenced by your prior experiences

with people and the types of behavior you have come to expect from them. If you think that people find you uninteresting, chances are you will be looking for signs in the therapist that he/she is bored with what you are talking about. You might, for example, interpret a blank look as an expression of disinterest. Or you might notice a yawn that would go unseen by another client. This, of course, does not mean that it is not possible for your therapist to be bored and disinterested in you. It does suggest that if you see your therapist acting toward you in ways that you see everybody else acting toward you, the reason may lie in your tendency to focus on such behavior rather than on the therapist's true feelings about you. You have to separate your personal sensitivities to others from attitudes that are really there. This is what is known as "working out the transference feelings," although it could more aptly be called learning to perceive in broader perspective. Since you are inclined to relate to the therapist in the same way that you relate to other people, your feelings about the therapist are very important to bring up in the therapy sessions. From these exchanges you can learn the ways in which unrealistic perceptions restrict you in relationships with others. Since you will also have realistic perceptions of the therapist, the ways in which you may be misinterpreting must be clear to you. You should not accept a therapist's statement that your perceptions are distorted if this cannot be demonstrated to you in some tangible way. Either the therapist is incorrect, or he/she has not done a proper job of helping you understand.

Some people feel more strongly about their therapists than others. This relates partly to the type of person you are, partly to the type of person the therapist is, and partly to the intensity of the psychotherapy process. If you are generally an emotionally reactive person you will probably find yourself feeling intensely about the therapist as well. If you are reserved in your feelings it is likely that you will be that way toward your therapist. Similarly, different degrees of emotionality on the part of the therapist will modify your responses. The place therapy has in your life is also important. When you are deep into therapy, have frequent sessions, and find yourself focusing your life around the therapy sessions, you are going to become more involved in your therapist than a person for whom therapy plays a peripheral role.

When people compare notes about their therapists, it often happens that a client may feel disappointed to learn that others have very intense relationships with their therapists while they do not, or that others are "wild" about their therapists while they experience him/her neutrally. There is no "proper" way to feel toward your therapist and the feelings that do emerge result from the combination of you, the therapist, and the goals you set. Intense positive feelings to the therapist are no guarantee of good or better therapy. Positive feelings as well as negative feelings are restricting for you if they arise out of a need to see the therapist in a particular way and to maintain a set view of the world. You want to be open in therapy to experience the therapist as he/she is, not as you would prefer to have him/her. To be open to the therapist and to his/her flaws and limitations is basically a more positive experience than to be blindly swept away by unrealistic admiration or hate. Try to evaluate your therapy relationship in terms of its meaningfulness to you, not according to what your friends are experiencing.

The Therapist's Feelings About You

According to the traditional schools of thought, therapists are supposed to be impersonal and anonymous. The reason for the dictum against therapists revealing personal feelings or personal information about themselves is that the less the client knows about the therapist, the more one can understand distortions in the client's perceptions about the therapist; whatever is imputed to the therapist is then clearly a product of the client's feelings. Many therapists have come to recognize that they are not just a blank screen or mirror for the client but a living person who exudes feelings and sentiments even when just sitting quietly. A therapist cannot avoid an emotional relationship with a client but only deny it. Even aloofness is a form of emotional relationship. Since research has shown that successful psychotherapy depends on a genuine, warm, and empathetic therapist, it is hardly in keeping with psychotherapeutic goals to have a therapist who remains detached and indifferent. All therapists have feelings about their clients. Mature therapists are aware of their feelings and can keep them from interfering with their genuine concern for the clients; immature therapists either deny the existence of their feelings or put them above the needs of the client.

Therapists also tend to react to clients in the same way that they react to people at large. Therapists who are generally overbearing are also apt to be overbearing with clients. Therapists who are generally unsure of themselves as people will also be more sensitive to a challenge from a client. Therapists who are generally more comfortable with women will be more comfortable with women clients. Therapists who are very nurturing like dependent clients, while therapists who are authoritarian like submissive clients. You cannot expect a therapist not to have personal predilections, but you can expect a therapist to be aware of these feelings rather than to deny them and risk their coming to expression in an uncontrolled and possibly destructive way.

In addition to therapists' idiosyncratic feelings about clients, there are some fairly typical feelings that therapists hold toward clients. Therapists, like other people, tend to like clients whom they feel like them. Hostility in clients produces anxiety and hostility in the therapist, which often causes defensive behavior. Therapists will try to pacify, withdraw from, react with counterhostility, or "court" clients whom they perceive as having a negative attitude toward them. Less competent therapists have more negative attitudes toward clients than competent therapists. Therapists tend to be less effective when the problems experienced by their clients are similar to their own problems. Therapist feelings toward clients can also vary day by day. Research bears out that when the therapist is feeling good, he/she will be warmer, more genuine and more effective with the client than when feeling bad or beset by personal problems. The effects of transient moods of the therapist cannot be eliminated but they can be recognized rather than erroneously attributed to other aspects of the therapy.

There is a tendency among therapists to admit to their feelings but to put the burden of these feelings onto the client. That is, the therapist will talk about his/her feelings with the client but ask what it is about the client that produces these particular feelings in the therapist. Looking to the client's problems to understand the therapist's reactions is a valid and often fruitful technique but it can deny the therapist's role in the feelings he/she experiences. For example, if the therapist is sarcastic with the client, the therapist may ask, "What about this client makes me so hostile?" rather than putting the question, just as pertinently, "What about me makes me respond to this client in such a hostile way?" Because therapy is a relationship between two people, the therapist must ask both questions together.

One of the most problematic aspects of therapist feelings for clients involves sexual feelings. In their need to gain approval and acceptance by the therapist, clients may become sexually seductive. Sometimes therapists see clients who are openly eager for sexual relations as a form of reassurance that the therapist is interested in them. To complicate the situation further, many clients come to therapy with sexual problems and seek therapeutic help in becoming more sexually responsive. The therapist then finds him/herself sought after as a sex teacher and sexual object combined. Many therapists are themselves sexually attracted to a client and find it easy to rationalize their own sexual interest as a reaction to projected seduction, even when there is no sexual seductiveness on the part of the client. Since the majority of therapists are men, and the majority of clients are women, usually younger, the classic pattern of older admired man becoming sexually involved with younger admiring woman is often reenacted. The gossip about professors and their young female students or physicians and their young female patients finds its counterpart in tales about therapists and their young women clients. While there are no statistics on the extent of sexual intimacy between therapist and client, it has been openly acknowledged by many women clients, and some therapists—for example, Martin Shepard in *The Love Treatment*—openly profess a belief that such sexual encounters may be beneficial. There is good reason to believe that a lot more therapists engage in sexual intercourse with their clients than are willing to admit it: while within the therapy they may promote such activity as being in the client's best interest, they are quick to deny to anyone outside that they have engaged in sexual activities, thereby belying their own statements to the client. The profession of psychotherapy itself does not help much in defending the rights of female clients from such behavior on the part of male therapists. Just as in cases of rape, there is a tendency among psychotherapists to hold the woman client responsible for sexual activity between her and the therapist, attributing it to her needs or seductiveness, and to require collaborative evidence that is unobtainable.

In her book *Women and Madness,* Phyllis Chesler reports on a variety of interviews conducted with women who had sexual relationships with their therapists, most with unhappy consequences. While it is understandable that sexual attraction between client and therapist can blossom in the intimate atmosphere of a therapy relationship, once the relationship becomes one of sexual intimacy it can no longer be a professional relationship. Undoubtedly contact with a warm and loving sexual partner can be therapeutic, but it is not psychotherapy. If a client and therapist have such strong feeling and attraction for each other, it is time to terminate their therapy contract. Perhaps the most abusive aspect of sexual relations between psychotherapist and client is the practice of charging for "sessions." In such circumstances, it would seem that whatever professionalism is left would be more aptly termed prostitution than psychotherapy.

9.
Resistance or Incompatibility?

WHEN YOUR THERAPY IS MOVING ALONG WELL, YOU will probably feel very positive about it. Therapy seems great when you are getting tangible help with disturbing problems or when you are caught up in the excitement of growing and changing.

Negative feelings about therapy are more significant and harder to track down. Negative feelings arise not only when the therapy is not working but, paradoxically, also when the therapy is working. It is easy to understand why you would feel antagonistic to therapy when something is going wrong. But why would you feel that way when it is going right? When therapy works, it means that you are uncovering and dealing with unpleasant aspects of your existence. It also means that you are coming face to face with alternative ways of living that both beckon and make you despair. While everybody who is committed to therapy wants to change, when therapy brings you to the point where the possibility of change becomes real, strong pulls emerge from within to keep you the way you are. Long-standing life-styles cannot be given up, even if they have caused much suffering, without the anxiety of losing the familiar and the fear of confronting the unknown. Abandoning old patterns of existence when you are not sure that you can make it any other way is a frightening prospect. When therapy brings you to this point, you may want to run from it. Since the idea of standing in one's own way of change is very difficult to accept, most clients attempt to prevent having to acknowledge it by fighting the therapy. This blocking of therapy to avoid its impact is called "resistance."

You cannot have successful therapy without feeling resistant at times. Resistance is a sign that therapy has brought you up against something important. Feelings of resistance are disturbing to both the client and therapist. They make the client feel guilty and the therapist feel frustrated. But these feelings are not to be condemned or shunted to the side. Understanding the fear that is creating the resistance can be the key to permitting you to face it and go on.

Because negative feelings about therapy can arise when the therapy is working as well as when it is not, it is important that you determine where such feelings are coming from. If you start to feel annoyed with therapy or angry at the therapist, you will start wondering: "Is it all my problem or is there something wrong with the therapist? Am I resisting or do I have a legitimate complaint?" These doubts can become very problematic and need to be ironed out with the therapist. Unfortunately, a lot of clients don't have the wherewithal to bring up critical feelings; that's why they're in therapy. Those who can brave it out and talk about their doubts aren't always successful either in clarifying their feelings, for they frequently meet with the pat phrase, "You're resisting." The therapist may point out that focusing on therapist inadequacies is a way of avoiding looking at the client's own inadequacies, or that the client characteristically reacts in an accusative and hostile manner when getting close to someone. While most therapists are very quick to see the client's resistance to continuing therapy, a lot are much slower to explore their own role in client dissatisfaction. Clients do resist therapy but it also happens that therapists can be unsuitable or just plain incompetent. A good therapist recognizes that when a client raises questions about the therapist's competence, more may be at stake than resistance. It should be obvious to the therapist, as it is to the client, that something is going on that needs to be explored. Only a defensive therapist will take such questions as a personal threat or view them primarily as a vehicle for the client's aggression. Trying to hurt the therapist and get in a couple of good licks is a popular game among clients, but a competent therapist will seek to explore with the client what is at the root of this need to hurt the therapist, and often it is something that the therapist has done or said. For a therapist to admit to his/her role in arousing the client's anger is not necessarily to attest to incompetency; if he/she has made an error in judgment, it remains to be seen whether it is of such magnitude that it will interfere with the future productivity of the therapeutic relationship.

When clients become distressed about shortcomings in their therapy and are intimidated about discussing these feelings openly with the therapist, they frequently try to clarify such problems with friends. This also tends to be labeled as a form of resistance. Freud originally formulated the view that any outside discussion of the therapy was an indication of resistance, and this view is still held by some therapists. Justification for such a view exists only if the client does not bring these issues up for discussion with the therapist.

Since the question of resistance is a crucial one and since many therapists are touchy when you question the therapy, below are some guidelines to help you distinguish between negative feelings stemming from resistance and negative feelings stemming from shortcomings in the therapist.

Signs of Resistance

If you find yourself falling into the following types of situations, you may well be dealing with resistance.

- When everything in the therapy was going alone fine, but then suddenly it seems to turn sour.
- When you've been with several therapists and find yourself repeatedly coming up with the same kinds of dissatisfactions.
- When the dissatisfactions with the therapist are similar to those with other important people in your life.
- When sudden attitude changes occur toward things affecting the therapy, such as finding the therapy is costing you too much time or money, or becoming convinced that therapy doesn't really work.
- When the press of other activities makes you cancel or forget your therapy appointments.

- When you keep the therapist in the dark about relevant issues in your life.
- When you start thinking about terminating therapy way before you had originally planned.
- When there's nothing specific you dislike about your therapist but you have an overwhelming impulse to flee.

While wanting to quit therapy is the most blatant way that resistance expresses itself, these other reactions are indirect ways of withdrawing from the therapy. If you are not aware of any resistance on your part but your therapist tells you that you are being resistant, do not reject such a suggestion out of hand. Your therapist should be prepared to discuss with you the behavior on which his/her view is based, and the explanation should be plausible to you.

Signs of Incompatibility

Since the bias in the therapist's attitude tends to be toward interpretations of resistance rather than acknowledgment of realistic discontent, it is helpful to have as well some basis on which to evaluate your therapist's role in making you unhappy with therapy. Certain types of behavior on the part of the therapist suggest that your negativism is being caused by an unsuitable therapist rather than by your resistance to the therapy process. Clear and direct feelings that the therapy is not being helpful are more likely to be indicators of questionable therapy than are indirect feelings of which you are less aware. Here are some situations which suggest that the fault lies with the therapist or therapeutic relationship rather than with you.

- When the therapist is not your type of person. Therapy is difficult enough without burdening it further with a lack of rapport. If you and your therapist were not meant for each other, it may be futile to try to stay together. Sometimes you feel right from the beginning that you don't make a good pair, sometimes that doesn't strike you until later. Maybe you sense the therapist as ungenuine and stereotyped. Maybe he/she is pretentious and stuffy—throwing big words around, or trying to impress you with his/her important clients. Perhaps he/she is just plain dull and limited—he/she can't understand a literary allusion, thinks a madrigal chorus is a rock group and that *Playgirl* is a magazine for liberated women. Perhaps the therapist has other qualities that turn you off and make you wonder about how well he/she is put together: obesity, chain smoking, nervous twitches, very fussy or overly casual dress, bleached hair, et cetera. Whatever the complaint, if you're on different wave lengths you'll both have trouble tuning in clearly to each other's messages.

- When there is a value conflict. Very often, barriers to therapy are created by a divergence in basic values between you and the therapist. Mutual respect for each other's ethics, style of life, and future goals, whether in or out of therapy, are prerequisites for a productive relationship. The therapist may be too conventional in outlook and frown on your search for new ways to fulfill yourself, or he/she may indiscriminately swing with each new fad while you are looking for more meaningful and lasting experiences. Perhaps the therapist is a sexist who belittles your struggle to establish your sense of self-worth as a woman. Or, perhaps, the therapist feels your radical politics are nothing more than an adolescent rebellion. If you don't accept the therapist's values, or feel that he/she pooh-poohs yours, you'll have a tough time making a go of it.

- When your therapist is a cold fish. If you experience the therapist as too cold or aloof, you may not be receiving the kind of emotional warmth that is needed for relationships aimed at personal growth. While the purpose of therapy is not to provide you with a new friendship, a friendly and responsive atmosphere helps you mobilize your strengths. A therapist may try to mask an inability to extend him/herself to you by labeling his/her behavior as professional distance. Such emotional detachment may not, however, be serving your interests as much as his/her defenses.

- When your therapist is a "star." It is very exciting to be "in" with a therapist who has flair, who sparkles, and who exudes "personality" and charm. Such magnetism can easily turn into hero worship, however, and become overpowering. While it is easy to get started with a very expressive therapist, and to become fascinated by his/her charisma, in the long run such an influence can be stifling. An intense, personal relationship with such a therapist can rob you of your autonomy and, perhaps more dangerously, your objectivity about what is going on. Some therapists exist as a type of guru and feed on the admiration of their cultists. Excessive devotion to the therapist subverts the quest to find power and value within yourself.

- When your therapist is hung up on unimportant areas. If the therapist repeatedly encourages you to discuss issues that don't seem particularly relevant to you it may be because his/her needs are overshadowing yours. Sometimes a therapist may spend much of the session pressing you for details of your childhood, a dream, or a personal encounter. Or the therapist may want details on a party, a play, or some other event you may feel is not important. In these cases, the value of such probes may be only in feeding a therapist's need for theory confirmation, or for gossip or vicarious excitement. If you feel your therapeutic time could be spent to better advantage, it probably could.

- When your therapist is hung up on you. You might sense that your therapist is overly involved in you personally rather than as a client. He/she may be jealous of your other interests or relationships and become critical of your attempts to move out into the world. In extreme cases, a therapist's needs get played out in more active abuses of clients such as inducing a client to have sex with him/her under the guise of liberating the client's blocked ability to love, be intimate, or have orgasms. To maintain control of a client, some therapists threaten dire consequences if you want to leave the relationship: "You'll become an alcoholic again."; "You'll fall apart." The main threat is, however, remaining locked into such a manipulative relationship.

- When your therapy is in a rut. If you find your sessions becoming increasingly uneventful and face them as another chore to be gotten through, something is wrong. Perhaps you are both tired, bored, or disillusioned, and the therapist is unable to find a different approach to which you can respond. Perhaps your therapist feels that your problems are so ingrained that he/she sets the goals too low. For example, the therapist may regard you as so basically passive and unresponsive that he/she doesn't try hard enough. Conversely, perhaps you have advanced to a level of feeling that places greater demands for emotional intensity on your therapist and he/she may lack the emotional competence to face up to your newfound strengths and independence. While the therapist was adequate before, he/she may no longer measure up to the job and back off from the confrontation you seek.

• When you feel down on yourself after therapy sessions. If you leave sessions feeling depressed and more displeased with yourself than before, this sense of dissatisfaction may be coming from an inadequency in your therapy. As in any other relationship, there is always a possibility that the interaction with the therapist may be inherently damaging rather than constructive. Your bad feelings may stem from disappointments with the therapy or the way you are allowing yourself to be treated within the therapy situation. Of course, many depressive feelings that emerge in sessions have nothing to do with the therapist, and may even reflect the problem that brought you to therapy in the first place. But you should distinguish between those downs that brought you into the therapy, and those that you take away from it.

• When you feel forced into a mold. Another way the therapist's needs can intrude into therapy is by his/her encouraging you to react and respond in ways that do not seem right for you. Therapists often feel that they know best, and see their role as getting you to accept this. The therapist's need to maintain control over you and to preserve status as the authority may push you into uncomfortable corners. For example, the therapist may expect you to be compliant and cooperative as a sign of your "adjustment." Refusal to accept an interpretation about yourself becomes a sign of your "resistance." Arguing the point with the therapist becomes further proof of your guilt (by revealing the depths of your resistance). Your need for independence is seen as negativism toward the therapist. Acquiescence on your part, while ostensibly for your benefit, may really be working against you.

- When you both behave in destructive ways. Sometimes therapy becomes an unending series of senseless arguments, blame-throwing sessions, or attempts to tear down each other's sense of self-respect. If the destructiveness cannot be resolved, it indicates a failure in the relationship. Such blaming and accusativeness often stem from a disillusionment of client with therapist or vice versa. If either one has unrealistic expectations of the other (which should not have been allowed to flourish in the first place), failure for them to materialize leads to frustration and anger. Like the child who finds the idealized parent is really weak, or the parent who finds the unrealistically appraised child is not a genius, the disillusioned client or therapist can find frustrated expectations turning into deep resentment.
- When your therapist is inconsiderate or selfish. Many clients feel annoyed at certain ways the therapist acts or at certain things he/she does, but accept these as occurring naturally in any therapy. Inconsiderate behavior, however, not only is unnecessary but should not be tolerated. While occasional lapses can be overlooked in a therapist as in anybody else, repeated occurrences should not be accepted. Some frequent abuses clients needlessly take for granted are: cutting sessions short, changing or not keeping appointments, reading mail or falling asleep (yes, this really happens), rigid refusal to discuss a problem on the telephone, inflexibility in charging for missed hours, lack of concern for your immediate problems (job demands, family needs, sickness) that interfere with maintaining regular therapy appointments, or unreasonable demands on you in terms of fees or time

of appointments. Also to be questioned are objection-
able personality traits that repeatedly manifest themselves, such as excitability, belligerence, defensiveness,
argumentativeness, sarcasm, lack of patience or sense
of humor. Your therapist should, at the very least, be
able to treat you with the ordinary respect and cour-
tesy due another human being.

• When your therapist won't discuss your doubts. One
indication that therapy is not working out is a therapist's refusal to discuss your doubts about the therapy.
If you should bring up any of the above points, or
want to talk about any other doubts or discontents and
the therapist refuses to do so, then his/her adequacy
as a therapist is suspect. Some therapists may let you
ramble on, but then become very defensive and/or
accusative. Perhaps, most telling of all, some therapists
may angrily reject you, telling you, "If you don't like
it here get out!" If that should happen, it is probably
the best advice the therapist has ever given you.

You can, and should, discuss these issues with your
therapist, but if such discussions get you nowhere, you are
still left with the job of making a decision as to what is causing your displeasure with therapy. Sometimes an outside
opinion is useful. You can go to another therapist to consult
about your quandaries but here, too, you must be on guard
against biases. Some therapists are prone to see the therapist as always in the right, while others are happy to help
you find fault with your therapist because that gives them a
sense of superiority over their colleagues. Other biases might
exist about the particular type of therapy you are in or
about the professional training of your therapist (whether
medical or psychological). More recently, the gender of the
therapist has become an issue, with some female therapists
decrying the influence of male therapists on female clients and
with some male therapists objecting to the "unfeminine" di-
rections set by feminist therapists for clients of the same sex.
Of course there are therapists who will be able to help you clarify your feelings and the issues involved without biases clouding
the picture. The point is, it is just as important that you exer-

cise discretion in choosing a consultant and accepting his/her interpretations as it is when you choose a therapist. You might also try discussing your problem with an informed friend. Getting playback from a person you respect and who has no vested interest in the situation may help you clarify your feelings and reformulate your own thinking.

Ultimately you, and only you, have to be the one to decide whether or not you and your therapist are incompatible. Don't be afraid to listen to your own feelings and use your own judgment; if you sense that things are going wrong, you are probably right.

10.
Terminating Therapy

HOW DO YOU KNOW WHEN IT'S TIME TO STOP THERAPY? The obvious answer is that you terminate when you reach your goals. The problem with this answer is that few people have goals that are so specific. If you do come to therapy to overcome a particular symptom or problem, then knowing when to terminate is relatively easy. But if you come to therapy because you want to grow and become freer as a person, then the decision becomes more difficult because there is no clear ending to personal development. The decision to terminate therapy in that case is not based on reaching a perfect solution to your problems but in having developed the ability to keep growing and searching on your own.

Realization of Readiness

The realization that you are ready to terminate therapy comes about gradually. A variety of changes take place in you that, after a while, add up to the feeling that you are ready to go it alone. No two people experience this the same way, but some typical changes are appreciating the good things about yourself, becoming able to see things more clearly, having a greater sense of confidence, and being more open to feelings. You become able to let go of past hurts and realize that future satisfying relationships are possible and attainable. You feel ready to embrace life more fully and tolerate the anxieties that are part of an open encounter with life. With the assimilation of these gains, the principle of diminishing returns sets in: you realize that the burdens of therapy, the

161

time, effort, and money involved, are starting to outweigh the benefits.

As you begin to change and feel your own power, you will also start to notice changes in the relationship between you and the therapist. The therapist will become more and more like any other person to you. You will be able to recognize your therapist for what he/she is and not approach him/her with awe or with unrealistic expectations. You will be able to accept his/her limitations without feeling angry or betrayed. You will find it easier to confront the therapist, you will be able to tell the therapist when you think he/she is wrong, and you will be able to disagree without questioning yourself first or worrying about the consequences. You will find that you have become more genuinely active in your sessions and have taken on more and more the role of the therapist. You will look less for guidance, realize there is less work to do, and find time to share more information and laughter together. You will be able to think of the idea of separation without becoming panicky and wondering what will become of you. Finally, you will start feeling somewhat restless in coming to therapy and wonder if it isn't time to quit.

How to Terminate

Termination is not a specific act, but a phase of therapy. The first aspect of termination is to clarify your reasons for wanting to terminate and to explore for resistance as well as for positive indicators. Once you have reached a decision to terminate, hopefully with the therapist's concurrence, set up a time so that your remaining work can be done with a specific end date in sight. Part of the ending period is used for reviewing and integrating what has gone on in therapy. It is helpful to tie up the loose ends and know where you are, where you want to go, and the resources you have to rely on. During this period you will want to do as much of the therapeutic work as possible, not only because you are ready to be your own therapist, but to help you experience that power in yourself. The therapist's role during termination is not so much to be a therapist as to make sure that you become aware of any tendency to leave that job to someone else.

Setting aside a specific time period for termination also

has the advantage of getting you and the therapist used to the idea of separation. When your termination date is fixed and you both know you are winding up, it helps you become accustomed to the idea of no longer having the relationship.

Sometimes, people prefer to terminate therapy by spacing out sessions at greater and greater intervals. They do not set a final date but wind down gradually. This might be a preferable way to stop if you are unsure of how well you will be able to manage on your own. It gives you an opportunity to work things out by yourself with only occasional visits back. This is generally a more appropriate way to terminate therapy that has been oriented toward helping you with a particular crisis or problem rather than with therapy oriented toward uncovering and growth. In spacing out termination it is important to guard against letting the therapy linger on indefinitely. Supportive visits spaced out at monthly intervals can themselves become an interminable affair if both therapist and client are not careful to work toward a cutoff point.

If you have qualms about your decision to terminate you may suddenly find new problems or experience old problems with an urgency you did not have before. While you can pinpoint new areas you still want to work on, your final sessions are not the time to start that work. Termination is a time for integrating what has been accomplished, not for opening up new problem areas. When you have terminated, you may find that these problems do not seem as awesome as they did before and that your temporary panic has dissipated. Remember, if you do find that you cannot resolve these problems without help you can always return to therapy in the future. But first, give it a try on your own.

Who Should Propose Termination

You are the best judge of when to terminate and that decision should rest with you. While some clients are prone to wait for the therapist to suggest that it is time to terminate, it is really up to the client to know when he/she is ready. In fact, the therapist may wait for you to bring up this issue as a sign that you are ready to leave. The best situation, of course, is when the client and therapist mutually agree that the time is ripe to end therapy, but this does not always happen. Often, the client wants to leave and finds that the therapist disputes his/her readiness to do so. This creates a difficult situation for the client who then has to gain the therapist's approval, leave without it, or stay in therapy without being committed to doing so.

If you feel you are ready to terminate and the therapist disagrees, it is up to the therapist to point out and discuss with you the reasons why. Since resistance is an inevitable phenomenon in psychotherapy, it often happens that clients have a desire to flee when they come face to face with more difficult problems. The therapist's function is to help you clarify your need to terminate at that particular point and to present in a straightforward manner what he/she considers the drawbacks to termination. Some therapists, if they have very strong feelings about a client's termination, either because they fear that it may be dangerous for the client or because of their own needs, try to sell clients on the benefits of remaining in therapy. Others arouse client anxieties by predicting relapses as a result of terminating. Although the therapist may be correct in his/her predictions or reasons, he/she should not try to force you into staying any more than to make any other decisions for you. The therapist's responsibility is to clarify what is involved in your decisions, but he/she must leave them up to you. When you and the therapist remain at odds, and you find it difficult to evaluate the situation, it is a good idea to consult with another therapist.

Premature Termination

People often stop therapy before they have reached their goals or have approximated the possible benefits. Such premature terminations may be brought on by either the client or the therapist. Premature client terminations occur for a variety of reasons, some good and some bad. As discussed in chapter 9 ("Resistance or Incompatability?"), sometimes you have to terminate therapy because you are in an unproductive or destructive therapy situation. You might also want to terminate prematurely when you are in productive therapy because of resistance to change, and guidelines for assessing such resistance have already been given. Sometimes, when people are afraid of what the therapy may uncover, they find that they suddenly lose their symptoms and start to feel fine. This "flight into health" occurs because the person finds it easier to relinquish a particular symptom than to relinquish the defensive system on which it is based. In such a situation, the flight into health is rarely permanent and symptoms or distress usually reappear in short order. Some people terminate prematurely because they despair of ever being helped and they just give up even trying. Both extreme despair and a flight into health, while evidencing the client's resistance to change, also indicate that the client does not have enough faith or trust in the therapist to help him/her through the struggle. Conversely, another reason for premature termination is the unwillingness to let another person be helpful. People who find it difficult to enter therapy because they are afraid of becoming dependent on the therapist are apt to terminate prematurely to nip the possibility of such dependence in the bud. They want to make sure that they can manage everything on their own and do not like to acknowledge the need for others. Some clients terminate prematurely as soon as they have made some tangible progress. They are not dissatisfied with the therapy; rather, their gains make them overly optimistic and they leave therapy out of elation at what they have accomplished, but before they have gotten fully into it.

Premature terminations fostered by the therapist are similarly motivated by good and bad reasons. Sometimes a therapist will suggest early termination because he/she feels realistically unable to help the client any longer. The therapist may feel that his/her particular way of working is no longer suited to the client's needs or temperament or that he/she just does not know how to meet the client's needs. In such a case the therapist might suggest that the client terminate their relationship and continue therapy with someone else. Although such a suggestion is apt to be experienced as a rejection by clients, it is offered in their best interests. A therapist might also suggest a temporary break in therapy to give a client time off to assimilate what has been going on and to consolidate gains. In this case, the termination is also suggested in the interest of the client.

It also happens that therapists encourage termination

because of their own needs. A therapist might start to feel very uncomfortable with a client whose progress is slow because that makes the therapist feel inadequate. The therapist may then exaggerate signs of progress to convince him/herself and the client that the therapy has been successful and suggest termination before the client is ready. Therapists may also terminate prematurely because they basically don't like a client and just don't want to work with him/her any longer. It could be that the therapist did not realize the extent of this dislike at the outset of therapy or that he/she needed to fill the time and decided to put up with the client until a "better" one came along. If a client, or the client's problem, is experienced by a therapist as very threatening and the therapist is not able to tolerate these anxieties, the therapist might suggest termination, using a variety of excuses. Even if a client does not upset the therapist, but the relationship just does not satisfy his/her needs, the therapist may want to replace that client with another who is more readily accessible to his/her influence or more admiring. Sometimes therapists terminate prematurely for reasons unrelated to the therapy process: they want time off to write a book, to see a higher-paying client, to cut down their hours, or any one of a number of personal reasons. When clients are rejected for such reasons, therapists rarely acknowledge them and try to put the responsibility for ending therapy on the client by suggesting the client is unmotivated, too resistant, or "not a candidate for psychotherapy." Such a rejection does not reflect on you. Although it is painful, you must keep in mind that it comes from the therapist's problems rather than from yours.

Delayed Termination

As with premature termination, termination may be delayed by either the client or the therapist for a variety of reasons. Clients delay termination when they are unduly afraid they cannot make it without the therapist's help. Sometimes, even after they become aware of the desire to leave, they suddenly revert to unproductive patterns of behavior as a way of convincing both themselves and the therapist that they are not yet ready to go. Clients also become addicted to therapy, afraid to face life without their weekly "fix." When termination is delayed for such reasons, it is usually because the client's dependency needs or the therapist's need to maintain control have not been worked out. It is very hard to terminate if you are getting the message from the therapist that he/she feels you have not attained sufficient strength to be on your own. Some persons, while realizing they are ready to leave therapy and able to handle the problems they came in with, fear that they may not have the resources to deal with new problems that arise. In such a case, it is up to the therapist to help the client make the break, with the understanding that it is always possible to come back and get help if and when necessary.

Occasionally therapy is prolonged because of side benefits. If a client has been using therapy as a way to obtain special indulgences from others ("What do you expect from me—you know I'm in therapy."), he/she may be unwilling to give up these secondary gains. In such a case, this need to garner attention or excuses is itself a problem that the therapy could still profitably work out.

Some clients delay bringing up termination because they are afraid of offending the therapist. Therapists sometimes do feel rejected if a client wants to leave. The therapist may feel guilty that the client will leave before the therapist has "finished the job" or because he/she is afraid that the client wants to leave because the therapist has not been effective enough. Although you may be correct in expecting that your therapist will be upset with your leaving, this is no reason to delay terminating. You have to leave when you are ready: you are not in therapy to work out the therapist's problems.

Therapists may also try to delay termination. A therapist may want to hold on to a client because that person has some particular quality that is attractive. For instance, quite a few clients come from glamorous worlds—the theater, broadcasting, politics, publishing—since generally these are the people with enough money to pay for therapy. For many a therapist whose private world is rather drab by comparison, having a relationship with such a worldly figure becomes a vicarious route to participating in the exciting goings-on. Such a client may also be the therapist's entree to other prominent clients. Therapists have a tendency to evaluate their status according to the status of their clients, so that letting an "important" client go can mean a loss of personal prestige as well.

One of the most obvious reasons for keeping a client in therapy longer than desirable is financial. On the average, a client who comes twice a week represents a fee of about $3,000 a year. If there isn't another client on the waiting list, that's a big chunk of income walking out the door. If the therapist is open and responsible, he/she will face it and not let it stand in the way of indicated termination. But if such monetary anxieties are not recognized, the therapist might doggedly insist that the client stay in therapy, without looking at why the client wants to leave, since that would necessitate dealing with his/her own concern over the money.

A therapist may also be unwilling to let a client go because of his/her positive involvement and personal growth needs. A client, to a therapist, represents a lot of time and effort. A therapist gets involved in a client's progress as a writer gets involved with a manuscript, a chemist with an experiment, or a mathematician with a complex equation. Once a therapist gets drawn into the client's problems and into the client as a problem, it is difficult to let go for the simple reason that people don't like to leave engrossing work half done. There is a drive for completion, a drive for resolution, a desire to polish things off and to create something whole and beautiful. Any therapist with any degree of involvement with his/her clients is apt to feel that his/her work is being taken away without a chance to finish up if the client leaves too soon. When a therapist is engaged in a client's therapy to the point where his/her own growth processes are stimulated, giving up the relationship also means losing that avenue for the therapist's own development.

Still another reason a therapist may want to keep a client in therapy are the feelings he/she develops for the client over time. When a therapist becomes genuinely fond of a client, it is natural that he/she doesn't want to lose the relationship. When such a person leaves, the therapist loses more than just another client.

Perhaps the most common reason for delaying termination involves both client and therapist. Each may experience a sense of loss and sadness at having to end a relationship that has been intense and meaningful. Unable to bring themselves to part, the client and therapist drag out the therapy even though there is nothing much to be accomplished any longer. When these feelings of affection and mutual unwillingness to sever ties are openly acknowledged, the separation becomes easier to bear. Facing these feelings and being able to live with the loss is, in a way, the ultimate test of the therapy.

Unplanned Termination

Sometimes, even though you might not want to, you have to terminate therapy for reasons extraneous to the therapy. This might be necessitated by a sudden drop in your income, a move to a new location, a long-term illness. When you find that you can no longer come to therapy, it is a good idea to explore with the therapist the factors involved. Even though external events occur that make it difficult to continue, sometimes clients use these happenings as a way of leaving therapy when they do not want to face their own resistance to continuing. For example, if a loss of a job means you cannot pay your fee, do you announce your intention to quit before discussing the possibilities of a lowered fee with the therapist? Or, if you have to relocate, are you looking into the possibilities of a therapist at your new location? While you are free to quit for any reason you want, make sure that you are aware of your real reasons for doing so and not hiding them from yourself.

When you have to terminate for reasons beyond your control, you may experience this as a real loss. Hopefully, the break will be temporary. In the meantime you can try to continue on your own, exploring your feelings and being more open with yourself. Perhaps you can continue to have intermittent contact with your therapist, if not in person, by mail.

Therapists may also terminate the therapy for reasons external to the therapy. In such instances clients always feel rejected and, in fact, they are since the therapist is saying that other things in life are more important than continuing the relationship with the client. The therapist should be prepared to tell you why he/she has to terminate and to give you advance notice. Since you might have strong feelings about the therapist's leaving, he/she should make sure that you have the opportunity to express them fully. If you request help, the therapist should be prepared to suggest a replacement.

In unplanned terminations, as well as in planned ones, it is a good idea to use the last sessions to tie up loose ends by summing up work done and work remaining.

Chronic or Interminable Therapy

It is difficult to decide when to terminate therapy even when you sense you have made progress and are close to becoming the kind of person you want to be. But knowing whether or not to terminate when you have been dragging on in therapy for years without satisfactory progress is even more difficult. How long should therapy go on? Some people accept therapy as a part of their lives and become chronic clients: they may have put in ten or twenty years in therapy and are prepared to keep going even with no end in sight. Others put in many years but are troubled by the fact that they keep going and going. If a person feels he/she needs continued therapy, is it a good idea to keep it up indefinitely?

In part, the feeling that therapy drags on comes about from a false expectation that it should make rapid changes in a person's life. Many personal growth systems promise transformations in weeks or even weekends, and so the prospect of years of therapy seems a bit much by contrast. Yet to change one's way of life, to relinquish ingrained patterns, to search into the depths of one's soul, and to learn new ways of being must take time. There are no miracle cures. Sometimes people seemingly change overnight, and certain experiences do have profound effects. When such sudden changes do occur, it is usually because the groundwork has already been laid for change. Years of therapy may appear to have no effect but a concentrated growth seminar afterward may produce wonders because the soil was fertile. Thus "interminability" in therapy is often a product of faulty expectations.

Of course, it does happen that therapy drags on unduly. In some instances clients use never-ending therapy narcissistically, seeking to establish their complexity and specialness by virtue of the time required for the therapist to come to understand and know them. Although such clients could use therapy in order to come to terms with their poor self-image, the therapist should not allow interminable therapy to serve the needs for self-embellishment but confront those needs head-on. In such a confrontation, the therapist may have to insist on termination if the client wants to prolong it for ultimately self-defeating reasons.

Some clients who are stuck in the past and exceptionally resistant to change move at a frustratingly slow pace, making little progress over the years. Because of severe early deprivations and resentments, such clients just cannot give up the immature demand that life owes them something and has to make it up to them. They persistently reject taking responsibility for themselves and seek in therapy a way to balance the ledger rather than a way to close the account books. In such a situation there is serious question whether a person should continue in therapy indefinitely. After one has put in years working on the therapy and the results remain uncertain, there comes a point when he/she should terminate, ready or not. Staying in therapy may serve to strengthen the expectation that the pains and problems of living can be taken over by others. It may well be that venturing forth without supports may help one more to build on what has been accomplished. Despite the fears of going it alone, everybody sooner or later has to take the chance. This does not mean that one cannot look for help again, but first one should try it alone. If a person finds it necessary to reenter therapy, that is always open to him/her and new types of therapeutic experiences should be considered as possibly offering broader avenues for movement and change. Chronic clienthood not only saps the client's incentive to dare life on his/her own but also tends to sap the therapist's vitality or ability to work creatively with the client. If a client progresses slowly the therapist also finds little room to grow and may lose the feeling of challenge necessary for good therapy. Despite the therapist's guilt at "abandoning" a client who wants to continue on and on, it is usually the best solution.

Occasionally clients linger on indefinitely in therapy because of a continued need for external support when more appropriate sources are not available. For example, adolescents who come to therapy with behavior problems frequently find, once they get these sorted out, that there are no adult figures or other sources available for continued guidance. In such a case, the therapist, unwilling to leave the client in the lurch, takes on the role of guidance counselor and surrogate parent, and the so-called therapy becomes a long-range affair. Similar situations occur with disadvantaged persons who face a paucity of support services, with persons of limited inner resources who need continual guidance to function in a complex society, and with persons who through unusual circumstances find that there is no one available to serve as friend or companion. Despite the fact that the therapist can provide tangible help for these persons, such help is not psychotherapy. It is difficult for a therapist to refuse a client in need, but it is questionable whether a therapist should offer his/her services in such a setting. Offering guidance and companionship under the guise of therapy maintains the fiction that the client's problems stem from self-imposed limitations, whereas in reality they stem from shortcomings in the environment. Therapy should not obscure the truth; its ultimate job is to encourage people to face the truth of their situation and to help them modify it or learn to live with it. Every professional role has its limitations and a therapist cannot respond to all client needs at all times. A therapist who is truly committed to such clients would be of greater help by working for the establishment of necessary support services than by trying to offer such services him/herself.

Contacting the Therapist After Termination

Most clients operate under the assumption that it is not fitting or proper to contact their therapists after therapy is terminated. Although they often think of the therapist and would like to share information with him/her about certain events or accomplishments, they hesitate to do so, fearing that the therapist is no longer interested and would consider it an intrusion. If your therapy was successful, you should be able to follow your impulses in this regard and do what you feel like doing. Most therapists will be very pleased to hear from you and appreciative of your wanting to keep them posted. Aside from the genuine interest that one person develops for another after such close contact, therapists are interested in what happens to you because they have a lot at stake in your continued progress. How you make out and what you do when you leave therapy reflects in part how effective the therapist has been. It is less appropriate for the therapist to pry into your life after therapy is over and, for that reason, if any contact will be kept it will be up to you to take the initiative. If the therapist does not care about you once you are no longer his/her client, that is a loss for both of you. However, unless your parting has been unpleasant, don't deprive both of you by jumping to that conclusion.

11.
Starting Again

IF YOU HAVE HAD A BAD OR NONPRODUCTIVE THERAPY experience you will be faced with a dilemma. You will probably be drawn back to therapy to work out the problems that remain unresolved. But having been burned, you will probably be hesitant about trying it again. This is not an uncommon situation. Because of the hazards of the field, many people have suffered disappointment in psychotherapy and had to go looking again. Fortunately, the second stab at psychotherapy usually works out better than the first. The second time around you are more alert to shortcomings in the therapist and more focused on what you need in order to have successful therapy. In a sense, persisting until you find what you need is not really starting again, but continuing with an important task that you have committed yourself to undertaking.

People are not only drawn back to therapy after an unsuccessful try, but sometimes after a good therapy experience as well. Various circumstances can create a need for further therapy even when the first experience has been productive. Sometimes, if you leave therapy at the first signs of strength, you may not have had sufficient time to consolidate your gains. Sometimes it happens that after leaving therapy you find yourself coming up against new problems that you could not anticipate and which you feel you cannot handle on your own. It might happen that you find you cannot really progress as much as you would like or as much as you thought you would be able to, without help. Or, you might feel a desire to broaden out and work on more ambitious goals than you set the first time. Resuming therapy after good therapy can also be difficult.

Obstacles to Starting Again

When you are not able to get as much out of life as you want or find that problems are starting to bother you again, the thought naturally occurs to you to go back to therapy. If it helped you once, it should be able to help you again.

But this desire is often counterbalanced by a feeling that there is something wrong with you if you can't work things out on your own. Some people feel that once they have been in therapy they shouldn't need help anymore; admitting the need for help makes them feel like a failure. Sometimes one's friends and relatives may reinforce this feeling. They might mock the need for therapy as a sign of weakness and/or self-indulgence: "Oh, he can't live without a therapist."; "She needs somebody to make a fuss over her once a week."; "What's the matter with you—why don't you stop supporting a shrink and buy yourself a new suit?" To bolster the feeling that they are capable of managing on their own, these persons may not follow through with a desire to resume therapy.

It may also happen that as you feel a need for further therapy you start to feel angry at therapy. How come you need more therapy? If it really works why are you still troubled? You start to feel that the original therapy has let you down, that it didn't do enough for you. This anger might disillusion you about your prospects and turn you against the idea of going back to therapy.

If you are doubtful about the merits of starting again, it is often helpful to review where you were when you terminated. The optimism you felt at that time about your new-found strengths probably encouraged you to stop therapy even though you knew you were not a finished person—and could never be. There is no final point at which you are complete, there is no way to be problem-free, and there is no way not to experience anxiety, unless you are dead. It is not necessarily a sign of your weakness or of the inadequacy of your previous therapy that you once again find yourself coming across new obstacles and new problems. If your life were static and not progressing, there would be no new challenges to throw you off. The new crises that you meet—should you take that new job, should you break off that relationship—indicate that you are open enough to expose yourself to new risks and broader possibilities.

Therapists, too, often find subsequent rounds of therapy helpful. Freud was the first to insist that therapists periodically undergo reanalysis. One can never know oneself perfectly at any given moment since one is always in the process of evolving. To be totally open to oneself means, therefore, to be always reexamining oneself. Reentering therapy, for client or therapist, is a testament to one's unending search for self-responsibility and autonomy.

The Same or a Different Therapist?

Whether or not you will do better with the same therapist you had before or with a new therapist will depend on your previous relationship and what you are going back for.

If you are returning for a short-term consultation about a particular problem, or for a "booster shot," it is probably best to see the same therapist again. Being familiar with you and your needs, that person will be better able to help you in a short series of concentrated sessions.

If you are returning for extended psychotherapy, the choice of the same or a different therapist hinges on a number of considerations. When people have had an exceptionally good therapy experience they not only are drawn back to the same therapist but are often afraid to try someone new. They feel that no one else could possibly enable them to repeat the same kind of positive results. Such a feeling implies that the effectiveness of the therapy depends entirely on the therapist, and ignores that therapy can be productive only because of the combined efforts of you and the therapist. Given a competent therapist whom you like and respect, there is no reason why you cannot repeat your initial success. You might also feel drawn to the same therapist as before because you know his/her way of working and feel comfortable with a familiar situation where you know what to expect. It should be easier for you, however, to adapt to new ways of working and to new approaches once you already have been through a therapy experience. You may be somewhat afraid of the unfamiliar, but it does afford the opportunity for new perspectives.

If you have been with your previous therapist for a long time and want to develop new aspects of yourself, you are probably better off finding a new therapist. Each person, therapists included, has something different to offer and a slightly different way of looking at things, which help to enrich your experience.

In making a decision, it is helpful to ask yourself these questions:

- How well did you work with the previous therapist? Did you experience any barriers between you that you were not able to work through?
- Are your therapy needs now the same as before, or different?
- If they are the same, do you think that your therapist's approach still leaves room to shed new light on these problems? Do you think new perspectives or new techniques may make these old problems more accessible?
- If your needs now are different, how come these areas were not explored before? Were they left for the future or never considered? Do you think your former therapist's approach is suitable for your new goals? If not, do you feel your former therapist can work with you in different ways? Did your former therapist work with you the way he/she did because that was the most suitable for you at the time or because that is the only way he/she knew or felt comfortable with?

Sometimes clients want to return to therapy not because of new problems to work out but because there are unresolved aspects of the old therapy relationship. Perhaps there are deep feelings of affection for the therapist: you miss him/her a great deal and returning to therapy is the only way that you can think of to reinstitute the relationship. If you harbor angry feelings toward a former therapist or feel that he/she never really appreciated you, you may want to go back to therapy to tell the therapist off or to show him/her how well you have done. In these instances you will be drawn not to therapy, but to the former therapist. Be clear on what you want to accomplish and if you do not want therapy perhaps you can bring your feelings to resolution in a more direct way. If such feelings cannot be resolved, they may be an issue for therapy, but in that case, it would probably be best to work them out with a new therapist.

New Therapists

If you decide on seeing a new rather than the former therapist, the new therapist will, as a matter of course, want to talk to you about your former therapy experience. This is a responsible way to begin, providing a background and framework for the new work you will do together. You will want to talk about what brought you to therapy the first time, the goals you set for yourself, what you accomplished and were able to work out, what was most helpful to you in the therapy, how you felt about yourself when you left, and the reasons you want to come back to therapy. If the first therapy experience was unpleasant or unproductive there will probably be a lot of unresolved feelings remaining, which you will want to work through with the new therapist: how the experience affected you and how it made you feel about yourself and about therapy.

As a client resuming therapy you pose an extra challenge to the new therapist. There is a temptation for the new therapist in such a situation to want to do the job better than his/her colleague. Therapists, like other people, have their competitive instincts, but because they tend to work in isolation from their peers, they do not have much opportunity for playing these competitive needs out. Seeing somebody else's former client provides just such a situation. If you feel that the therapist is digging into the old relationship above and beyond what is useful, or that he/she is trying to show up your former therapist, this may be revealing a competitiveness and immaturity that does not bode well for the future of your new venture. Do not allow your new therapy experience to become the grounds for satisfying the unresolved needs of the therapist.

What Therapy Is Like the Second Time

Starting therapy again does not mean a boring repetition of the same old material. Just as in your previous therapy, you will find that some issues keep cropping up, but that as you review and rework them your perspective changes and the issues are experienced in a different way. Each time there may be something new to notice, some new configuration and repatterning that escaped you before. And, although there might be a lot of reworking to do, there will undoubtedly be a lot of new territory to cover as well. If you are in therapy with a new therapist then, of course, the different interaction between you two will also add spice to the proceedings. No matter whom you are with, therapy cannot be boring when you are growing and evolving.

Being in therapy a second time actually puts you at an advantage. Armed with your previous experience, you know how to use the therapy better and become a better client. You will find that you have more control of the therapy and will not have to rely so much on the therapist, but can use the therapist to help you focus more clearly on exactly what you want to do. As a more experienced client, you are more apt to avoid unproductive encounters and to get the best out of your therapist.

Suggested Reading

Politics, Conformity, and Psychotherapy

Clark, Ted, and Jaffe, Dennis T. *Toward a Radical Therapy*. New York: Gordon and Breach, 1973.

Halleck, Seymour L. *The Politics of Therapy*. New York: Science House, 1971.

Laing, R. D. *The Politics of Experience*. New York: Ballantine Books, 1967.

Slaby, Andrew, and Tancredi, Laurence. *Collusion for Conformity*. New York: Jason Aranson, 1975.

Szasz, Thomas S. *The Myth of Mental Illness*. New York: Harper & Row, 1961.

The Major Approaches

FREUD AND PSYCHOANALYSIS

Freud, Sigmund. *New Introductory Lectures on Psychoanalysis*. New York: W. W. Norton, 1933.

———. *The Basic Writings of Sigmund Freud*, edited by A. A. Brill. New York: Modern Library, 1938.

———. *A General Introduction to Psychoanalysis*. Garden City, N.Y.: Garden City Publishing Co., 1943.

ADLER AND INDIVIDUAL PSYCHOLOGY

Adler, Alfred. *The Practice and Theory of Individual Psychology*. New York: Harcourt Brace, 1924.

JUNG AND ANALYTIC PSYCHOLOGY

Jung, Carl G. *Modern Man in Search of a Soul*. New York: Harcourt Brace, 1933.

Jung, Carl G. *The Practice of Psychotherapy.* New York: Pantheon, 1954.

REICH AND VEGETOTHERAPY
Reich, Wilhelm. *The Function of the Orgasm.* New York: Orgone Institute, 1942.
————. *Character Analysis.* New York: Orgone Institute, 1949.

RANK AND WILL THERAPY
Rank, Otto. *Will Therapy and Truth and Reality.* New York: Alfred A. Knopf, 1947.

HORNEY AND THE CULTURAL APPROACH
Horney, Karen. *Neurosis and Human Growth.* New York: W. W. Norton, 1950.

SULLIVAN AND INTERPERSONAL RELATIONS
Sullivan, Harry Stack. *The Interpersonal Theory of Psychiatry.* New York: W. W. Norton, 1953.

ROGERS AND CLIENT-CENTERED THERAPY
Rogers, Carl R. *Client-Centered Therapy.* Boston: Houghton Mifflin, 1951.

EXISTENTIAL THERAPY
Boss, Medard. *Psychoanalysis and Daseinanalysis.* New York: Basic Books, 1963.
May, Rollo, Angel, Ernest, Ellenberger, Henri F., eds. *Existence.* New York: Basic Books, 1958.
Sonnemann, Ulrich. *Existence and Therapy.* New York: Grune & Stratton, 1954.

GESTALT THERAPY
Perls, Frederick, Hefferline, Ralph, and Goodman, Paul. *Gestalt Therapy.* New York: Julian Press, 1951.

LOWEN AND BIOENERGETICS
Lowen, Alexander. *Bioenergetics.* New York: Coward, McCann & Geoghegan, 1975.

JANOV AND PRIMAL THERAPY
Janov, Arthur. *The Primal Scream.* New York: G. P. Putnam's Sons, 1970.

Transactional Analysis
   Berne, Eric. *Games People Play*. New York: Grove Press, 1964.
   Harris, Thomas A. *I'm OK—You're OK*. New York: Harper & Row, 1969.

Ellis and Rational-Emotive Therapy
   Ellis, Albert. *How to Live with a Neurotic*. New York: Crown, 1957.

Family Therapy
   Ferber, Andrew, Medelsohn, Marilyn, and Napier, Augustus. *The Book of Family Therapy*. New York: Science House, 1972.

Child Therapy
   Axline, Virginia M. *Play Therapy*. Boston: Houghton Mifflin, 1947.
   Moustakas, Clark E. *Existential Child Therapy*. New York: Basic Books, 1966.

Group Therapy
   Klapman, J. W. *Group Psychotherapy*. New York: Grune, 1946.
   Rosenbaum, Max. "Group Psychotherapy and Psychodrama." In *Handbook of Clinical Psychology*, edited by Benjamin B. Wolman, pp. 1254–74. New York: McGraw-Hill, 1965.

Encounter Groups
   Lieberman, M. A., Yalom, I. D., and Miles, M. B. *Encounter Groups*. New York: Basic Books, 1973.
   Schutz, William C. *Joy*. New York: Grove Press, 1967.

Est
   Rhinehart, Luke. *The Book of est*. New York: Holt, Rinehart and Winston, 1976.

Hypnotherapy
   Wolberg, Lewis R. *Medical Hypnosis*. 2 vols. New York: Grune & Stratton, 1948.

Behavior Modification
   Bandura, A. *Principles of Behavior Modification*. New York: Holt, Rinehart and Winston, 1969.

Wolpe, Joseph, and Lazarus, A. A. *Behavior Therapy Techniques*. New York: Pergamon, 1966.

SEX THERAPY

Masters, William H., and Johnson, Virginia E. *Human Sexual Inadequacy*. Boston: Little, Brown, 1971.

MEDICAL TREATMENT

Walkenstein, Eileen. *Beyond the Couch*. New York: Crown, 1972.

Physician's Desk Reference. Oradell, N.J.: Medical Economics, published and updated annually.

Restak, Richard. "The Promise and Peril of Psychosurgery." *Saturday Review/World* September 25, 1973.

Kalinowsky, Lothar B. "Electric and Other Convulsive Treatments." In *American Handbook of Psychiatry*, edited by Silvano Arieti. 2d ed., Vol. 5, pp. 531–47. New York: Basic Books, 1975.

Feingold, Benjamin. *Why Your Child is Hyperactive*. New York: Random House, 1975.

Hawkins, David, and Pauling, Linus, eds. *Orthomolecular Psychiatry*. San Francisco: Freeman, 1973.

THE EFFECTS OF THEORETICAL APPROACH ON PSYCHOTHERAPY

Fiedler, F. E. "A Comparison of Therapeutic Relationship in Psychoanalytic, Non-Directive and Adlerian Therapy." *Journal of Consulting Psychology* 1950, 14:436–45.

Raskin, N. J. "The Psychotherapy Research Project of the American Academy of Psychotherapy." *Proceedings of the American Academy of Psychotherapy 1965:* 253–54.

Strupp, Hans H. "An Objective Comparison of Rogerian and Psychoanalytic Techniques." *Journal of Consulting Psychology* 1955, 19:1–7.

Wrem, R. L. "Counselor Orientation: Theoretical or Situational." *Journal of Counseling Psychology* 1960, 7:40–45.

Differences Among the Psychotherapy Professions

Burton, Arthur, and Associates. *Twelve Therapists*. San Francisco: Jossey-Bass, 1972.

Henry, William E., Sims, John H., and Spray, S. Lee. *Public and Private Lives of Psychotherapists.* San Francisco: Jossey-Bass, 1973.

———. *The Fifth Profession.* San Francisco: Jossey-Bass, 1971.

Rogow, Arnold A. *The Psychiatrists.* London: Allen and Unwin, 1971.

The Therapist's Personality

Aldrich, C. K., "Styles of Intervention." *Psychiatry and Social Science Review* 1967, 1:22–26.

Meltzoff, J., and Kornreich, M. *Research in Psychotherapy.* Chapter 12. New York: Atherton, 1970.

Swenson, S. C. "Commitment and Personality of the Successful Therapist." *Psychotherapy: Theory Research and Practice* 1971, 8:31–36.

Strupp, Hans H., and Bergin, A. E. "Some Empirical and Conceptual Bases for Coordinated Research in Psychotherapy." *International Journal of Psychiatry* 1969, 7:18–90.

Strupp, Hans H., Fox, Ronald E., and Lessler, Ken. *Patients View Their Psycho-Therapy.* Baltimore, Md.: Johns Hopkins University Press, 1969.

The Psychotherapy Contract

Adams, Sallie, and Orgel, Michael. *Through the Mental Health Maze.* Washington, D.C.: Public Citizen's Health Research Group, 1975.

The Psychotherapy Process

Singer, Erwin. *Key Concepts in Psychotherapy.* 2nd ed. New York: Basic Books, 1970.

Weiner, Irving B. *Principles of Psychotherapy.* New York: John Wiley & Sons, 1975.

Index